TRIALS OF TRUTH

TRIALS
OF
TRUTH

India's Landmark
Criminal Cases

PINKY ANAND
AND GAURI GOBURDHUN

Sdé

Shobhaa Dé
B O O K S

An imprint of Penguin Random House

SHOBHAA DÉ BOOKS

USA | Canada | UK | Ireland | Australia
New Zealand | India | South Africa | China | Singapore

Shobhaa Dé Books is part of the Penguin Random House group of companies
whose addresses can be found at global.penguinrandomhouse.com

Published by Penguin Random House India Pvt. Ltd
4th Floor, Capital Tower 1, MG Road,
Gurugram 122 002, Haryana, India

First published in Shobhaa Dé Books by Penguin Random House India 2017

ISBN 9780670089123

Typeset in Adobe Garamond Pro by Manipal Digital Systems, Manipal
Printed at Replika Press Pvt. Ltd, India

I dedicate this book to the cause of justice

CONTENTS

ACKNOWLEDGEMENTS

No man—or woman—is an island unto himself or herself. John Donne's famous words hold true for all times, including our own, and for almost all purposes, including this book, which makes an acknowledgements section not only proper but also necessary.

This book is the outcome not only of my own efforts but also of the support lent by a large number of people, the foremost of whom is my husband, Devendranath Goburdhun. His constant presence by my side and unwavering support in all my endeavours has been the reason why I could manage to do justice to most, if not all, of them.

If my husband has been a pillar of support at all times, my daughter, Gauri Goburdhun, has been the principal driving force. Without her, this book would have remained a mere idea.

I thank my mother, Padma Anand, for her support and encouragement, and I also thank the other members of my family for having been patient with me whenever I've been too busy to spend time with them due to my professional exigencies. Their support has been vital to the completion of this book—as crucial as the support they have unwaveringly extended so far for whatever else I have managed to successfully attempt in life.

I am grateful to Shobhaa Dé for being an inexhaustible source of support and inspiration to me.

I would also like to thank Milee and Roshini for their patience and for putting up with me through numerous missed deadlines.

Last but not the least—and not just in a manner of speaking, but sincerely—I extend my heartfelt gratitude to Saudamini, Karan, Devina and my entire office for tolerating the long working hours and untimely demands. I thank them for the countless times they adjusted and readjusted their schedules to accommodate the demands made on them.

In the end, I offer my special thanks to all those who do not find a mention here but who have contributed to my personal and professional life in their own big and small ways.

AUTHOR'S NOTE

As a lawyer and public figure, I have been fortunate to have had life-changing experiences. In the last thirty-five years, I have been witness to dynamic changes in laws and how these have impacted society and changed mindsets. As a woman, I have been fortunate to be a part of some of these trials, particularly those that have been watershed cases highlighting the issues of women's safety and crimes against my gender.

I see the law as a catalyst for the creation of an ideal society—not what is, but what it is supposed to be. This was taught to me and deeply inculcated in me by one of my Harvard Law professors. The idea that I could bring about change in the world became one of my primary motivations for becoming a lawyer.

My involvement with societal issues began early with a deeply ingrained sense of 'right'. As a law student, I was active in the Delhi University political scenario and became the first woman secretary to the Delhi University Students' Union. That experience further enforced the feeling that as a lawyer I could change our system from what it is to what it should be.

I think one of the many dynamic features that the interplay between people and the justice system has ensured is a reawakening of the concept of true justice and the re-emergence of the ideal of Satyamev Jayate—which translates to 'truth alone triumphs'. In particular, such learnings become apparent from cases such as those of Priyadarshini Mattoo and Jessica Lal. Perceptible changes that have come about with the involvement of civil society in controversial cases include dislodging the age-old perception that the high-profile accused will get away scot-free. Another case that changed the world as we used to see it was the Nirbhaya rape case, where the notion of crimes against women was revisited, leading to a paradigm shift in the ideas of victim shaming and blaming, and which led the way for more stringent laws, enforcement mechanisms and security. More importantly it brought to the forefront the way women felt, spearheading the thought process that they should not feel shame in being the victim and should in fact seek reparation and vindication for their suffering.

This book is my attempt to share how some of the cases that I was exposed to have changed society and, in certain cases, how society has effected the changes in law. Over the years I have realized that it is a two-way street when one sees the law as an instrument of change.

The inspiration for this book came to me when I met Shobhaa Dé at the ZEE Jaipur Literature Festival in Jaipur in 2016, where we talked about people's curiosity about legal cases, their desire to understand the nitty-gritty of legal provisions, to know what actually happened in the case, details about the persons involved in the crime, and their overall wish to understand how the system works and responds. This was a different approach, which excited and motivated me, and I readily proceeded to venture into this project.

However, this was not an easy task. As lawyers, we are used to discussing and analysing the contours of law with all its baggage. While complexity and technicalities are a part of the legal system, the challenge to make concepts palatable and interesting is another matter itself.

I have attempted this recording of my impressions over the years to try to provide an insight into how these cases have affected us and our collective thought process as a whole.

Criminal trials and their progress have always been subjected to intense public curiosity. The public wants to know what happened, why it happened and whether justice prevailed. Unlike civil trials involving money, property and service, criminal trials evoke public sentiment and emotion. I have seen civil society following each and every facet of a criminal trial, not just following but theorizing, analysing and opining. In some cases, the public's perception of appropriate justice is a far cry from jurisprudential justice.

These cases have resonated over the years and left an impact on us.

Each of the cases narrated has touched a chord within us.

One thread that runs through these chapters is that most of the crimes seem to be women-centric—be it Nirbhaya, Jessica Lal, Naina Sahni or Vidya Jain—thus shedding light on their extreme vulnerability.

Another recurring theme one can spot running through these cases is civil-society activism, by which we, as a whole, seek vindication for a crime that we adjudge to be gruesome or cruel. Although I admit that the criminal justice system does suffer from some inherent issues, like delays or failures in investigation, it is apparent that in cases where the criminal justice system falters, civil society takes up the cause, giving succour to the victims and ensuring that justice prevails.

This book is also my humble attempt to bridge the gap between lawyers and non-lawyers and to present a blow-by-blow account of the cases, unravel the real story, look beyond to the persons involved, the raison d'être, the societal impact and the course of justice.

Through these chapters I have attempted to set out my own growth as a lawyer over the years. My perception of justice and the impact that some of these cases left on me motivated me to try to make it a better world—not necessarily a (utopian) crime-free society but at least a world where justice was done and seen to be done.

Pinky Anand

1

FOR A FISTFUL OF RUPEES

The N.S. Jain murder case took the country by storm. As a young lawyer, it was the first trial I was attending at the Parliament Street district courts. The case was being tried by Ram Jethmalani, B.B. Lal and K.K. Luthra for the accused. I was fascinated. There was no direct evidence available. It was all about establishing links, typical to cases of contract killing. It was like fitting together the pieces of a jigsaw puzzle.

At the mention of contract killing, most people would instinctively think of trained professionals, slick and glamorous, in the style of James Bond, or the Jackal in Frederick Forsyth's *The Day of the Jackal*. The reality often is that contract killers belong to the poor sections of the society, exploited by vengeful people who don't want to dirty their hands and be nabbed for a crime. The problem with contract killing is that even if a trail is created, it is usually difficult to incarcerate the actual mastermind. Contract killers are ready to take on this risk for even a fistful of rupees, as little as Rs 500 at times. Organized-crime contract killing is slightly different; it is more gang-related and associated with violence around drug markets in large cities or trafficking transit zones in countries such as Brazil and Mexico. No matter the motivation, contract killers are emotionless, hard-hearted murderers who kill for cold, hard cash.

Crime lore has somehow managed to romanticize the entire gruesome process and merge it with ideas of honour and daring, but at the end of the day, it is nothing but an agreement to conspire and kill.

The entire process becomes a business transaction, instead of the emotionally fraught experience of actually committing a murder. Outsourcing the crime is always more beneficial for the hiring party, not only because they do not have to be directly involved, but also because it is difficult for law enforcement to employ traditional methods to determine guilt or motive, or establish circumstances. Often there is nothing to tie the contract killer to the victim and thus it becomes extremely difficult to link them. Simultaneously, the hirer can provide a watertight alibi for the time of murder and also ensure there is no visible money trail as all transactions are carried out in cash.

All these reasons put together have resulted in killing for hire becoming an entire terrifying industry in itself.

Over a period of time, contract killing has established itself as an expanding and growing business, with its own specific customs, sense of work ethic and norms such as anonymity and the importance of the reputations of the killers. Its dynamic base market, involving vast hosts of network and booming figures of supply and demand, has resulted in the creation of a massive nexus of nefarious intent and illicit activities. Single incidents are often indicative of an enormous operation that connects people across different spheres.

History of Contract Killing in India

Contract killing has been around as long as we can remember. Instances date back to when the kings or noblemen of the land used to hire killers to do their dirty work. During the 1960s and 1970s, the city of Bombay (now known as Mumbai) experienced the rise of the Indian underworld, the first-ever organized crime syndicate in the country. This notorious group of people and their lives have fed the fantasies of many a crime buff and made Dawood Ibrahim, Haji Mastan and Chhota Rajan household names.

The first reported case of contract killing in India was in 1969. The smuggler Haji Mastan paid two Pakistani men what was then a princely sum of Rs 10,000 to eliminate the gangster Yusuf Patel. However, this attempt was aborted.

Slowly, this set-up shifted to areas of Bihar and Uttar Pradesh since the Maharashtra police began conducting regular raids to eliminate these mafia power lords and sharpshooters. Unfortunately, in the former states, there were more people who could be easily convinced into being guns for hire due to the persistent poverty.

The mafia employed these men to get rid of powerful personalities—mostly in the realm of politics, the Indian film industry, real estate—or anyone else. They would do this to scare people into paying money to these overlords. Thus began a system of terror.

Another chilling case was the murder of the racketeer Amirzada Nawab Khan, carried out on the orders of Dawood Ibrahim. Khan was behind the murder of Dawood's elder brother, who had been shot in broad daylight at the Mumbai sessions court; he had been murdered by a twenty-four-year-old unemployed man, David Pardesi, for the price of Rs 50,000.

R.K. Sharma, an IPS officer, used to receive frequent visits from Shivani Bhatnagar in the Prime Minister's Office to gather information regarding matters on which she was reporting. These frequent meetings developed into intimacy, frequent phone calls and meetings after office hours. It is alleged that the couple were deeply in love with each other and Shivani was pregnant with Sharma's child. The relationship developed to such an extent that they decided to marry each other after divorcing their respective spouses.

The story as reported by the media was that by the time Shivani gave birth to a male child, Sharma, the appellant, had already lost interest in her. She threatened to ruin his life and career by exposing him but paid for it with her life. The contract killer Pradeep Sharma was identified, but R.K. Sharma himself was acquitted. The Delhi High Court examined whether Pradeep Sharma had murdered Shivani Bhatnagar. However, it was observed that even if this fact were established, it would further have to be proved that it was at the behest of someone else that Pradeep had committed the offence and not of his own free will, in order to establish a criminal conspiracy. Appeals against the acquittal of R.K. Sharma have been filed by the state in the Supreme Court and are pending.

One would imagine that in such situations, which involve the risk of incarceration and even the death penalty, the remuneration would be substantial. However, I have come across instances where some deals to commit murders are forged for as little as Rs 5000. While, on one hand, this reflects how morally depraved our society has become, on the other hand, it reveals some people's strong need for survival. The lack of basic education, services and skill sets in India, combined with greed and the low regard for human life, has turned committing murders into a viable job option.

A Pound of Flesh for Rs 25,000

Narendra Singh Jain's case marks the infamous 1973 contract killing of Mrs Vidya Jain. This case came to everyone's attention possibly because both the killer and the deceased belonged to the upper echelons of society. Somehow, when a murder takes place among well-to-do people, it has a higher impact on the public. In this case, the accused was Dr N.S. Jain, the personal eye surgeon of the then Indian President, V.V. Giri, who hired two people to kill his forty-five-year-old wife in conspiracy with his paramour, Chandresh.

The two questions that dominated the case were:

1. Which of the two—Jain or Chandresh, or both— took the final call to kill Vidya?
2. Did Jain really think that murder by unknown assassins would not give rise to questions? Would it be believable that Vidya had been murdered for no reason?

On 4 December 1973, Dr Jain came back to his house in the posh locality of Defence Colony in New Delhi at about 7.15 p.m. He asked his wife, Vidya Jain, to get ready so that they could visit his sister who lived in the same neighbourhood.

They were to go in their car, which was parked the house next door. A few minutes later, the couple came out of the house. As Dr Jain walked towards the right side of the car to open its door, his wife proceeded towards the left. Before he could unlock the door, he noticed that his wife was nowhere to be seen. He went around to the left side of the car and saw a figure lying prostrate in the nearby drain. Just then a man jumped out of the drain, brandished a pistol at Dr Jain and ran away along with another man towards the north.

Vidya's body was found in the ditch from which the assailant had emerged. She was pulled out of the drain with the help of some guests of the Jains and their domestic help. Vidya had suffered fourteen brutal knife injuries. She was bleeding profusely, so Dr Jain put her in the car and drove to a nearby nursing home, where she was declared dead on arrival.

A Meeting of Minds

The plan to kill Vidya Jain was extremely complicated and riddled with hiccups. Dr Jain had a paramour called Chandresh Sharma whom he was intimately involved with while being married to his wife. Together, they wanted to kill Vidya so that they could continue their relationship in the open. Chandresh knew Rakesh Kaushik, a twenty-five-year-old man working as an education havildar, whom she approached. Around September 1973, Rakesh got in touch with a man called Karan Singh with the proposal to kill the doctor's wife. Later, at another meeting, Chandresh accompanied Rakesh and gave Rs 1200 to Karan Singh and offered to pay Rs 20,000 for the entire operation, with Rs 10,000 given as an advance. On 14 September 1973, Chandresh took Rs 10,000 from her bag and gave them to Karan Singh. It is relevant that on the same day, Dr Jain withdrew Rs 10,000 in denominations of Rs 100. Karan Singh, however, invested the money in the purchase of a truck and never made an attempt on the life of Vidya Jain.

The second time they decided to hire someone for the murder, Rakesh went to his home town of Charkhi Dadri in Haryana and brought back twenty-year-old Ram Kishan, a motor mechanic. Rakesh was also acquainted with a taxi driver called Ramji. In November 1973, Chandresh told Ramji that she needed his taxi as she had a plan to kill

Dr Jain's wife and had arranged for a man to commit the act on her behalf. She promised him a car as a gift and an opportunity of permanent employment in return. After Ramji agreed to provide the taxi, Rakesh started threatening and coercing Ram Kishan to kill Vidya Jain. It seems that till this point Ram Kishan was unaware as to why he had actually been brought to Delhi. Ram Kishan pretended to cooperate with the trio for a while. He was arranged to be in Vidya Jain's proximity several times, but did not harm her. Ultimately, in December 1973, he concretely refused to kill her. Thus the second conspiracy to kill the doctor's wife also did not reach fruition.

Subsequently, Ramji took Rakesh and Ram Kishan to Kalyan Gupta. However, the chain of events and people did not end there. Ram Kishan was dropped at Bhogal in New Delhi, and Kalyan then took them to meet a man known as Bhagirath at the village of Ghori in Palwal district, Haryana. Bhagirath agreed to help them kill Vidya Jain and took them to Rajasthan to meet Ujagar Singh and Kartar Singh. A demand of Rs 25,000 was made by these two, which was readily agreed to.

From then on, the team of Ujagar Singh and Kartar Singh scoped Dr Jain's house several times.

The principal conspirators, broadly speaking, were Dr Jain, Chandresh and Rakesh. Chandresh and Rakesh were actively involved, while Jain seemed to take a back seat and exercise control from behind the scenes. The details of the conspiracy were discussed and a plan hatched at a bustling restaurant called New Vig

Restaurant in Chandni Chowk that Chandresh and Rakesh were known to frequent.

On 4 December 1967, Rakesh, at about 4.30 p.m., asked Ramji to accompany him to 'New Vig Restaurant' as 'the job' had to be done that day. They hired a taxi and went to Chandni Chowk. Chandresh, Bhagirath, Kalyan, Ujagar and Kartar were already present outside the restaurant. They went inside, and while they were drinking coffee and eating Dr Jain arrived. He talked to Ujagar, cautioning him to execute the job carefully. He also assured him that he would get the amount he wanted and that the case would also be taken care of. After Dr Jain left, Chandresh told the other conspirators that she would also be reaching Dr Jain's house in the doctor's car at about 6.30 p.m. She informed them that she would get down from the car outside the house, and instructed them that when the doctor emerged from the house along with his wife, Ujagar and Kartar were to kill her. She asked them to ensure that the doctor did not suffer any injury. From the restaurant, Ramji, Bhagirath and Kalyan left for Bhogal in a taxi and reached Defence Colony at about 5.45 p.m. Bhagirath and Kalyan went to the latter's house while Ramji returned to his jhuggi. The plan was executed later the very same evening.

No plan to commit a crime is ever foolproof. This case had several subplots, some of which failed. However, even though the final stages were meticulously planned, certain glaring features pointed the investigating agencies to Jain and Chandresh:

1. Robbery was not the motive. Nothing was stolen.
2. The crime was pre-planned.
3. Why was Dr Jain not attacked?
4. Why did Dr Jain not attempt to pursue the assailants? Why was he a mute spectator?

All these incriminating circumstances, coupled with the disclosure statement of Chandresh and Ujagar, concurrently pointed towards the guilt of Dr Jain.

When the police investigated, they found that Chandresh Sharma had been his secretary, whom he had fired to maintain peace at home. Chandresh was given a house by Dr Jain and regular cheques higher than her salary as his secretary were deposited in her account. It was established in court that Dr Jain and Chandresh wanted to marry each other and, therefore, conspired together to kill Vidya.

The trial court charged Dr N.S. Jain, Chandresh Sharma, Rakesh Kaushik, Bhagirath, Kalyan Gupta, Kartar Singh and Ujagar Singh under Section 120B of the Indian Penal Code, 1860 (IPC), for having entered into a conspiracy along with Ramji, the approver, to commit the murder of Vidya Jain and for murder.

Kartar and Ujagar were tried separately under Section 27 of the Arms Act for possession of the pistol and cartridges as also for the knife recovered from them. The sessions judge found Kalyan Gupta and Bhagirath guilty only for conspiracy while the rest were found guilty of all the charges against them and sentenced to imprisonment for life. Kartar and Ujagar were also sentenced to rigorous imprisonment for two years and one year respectively under Section 27 of the Arms Act.

Since there was only circumstantial evidence leading up to the event, the prosecution's task was a tough one. However, the prosecution, through the help of unprecedented efficient investigation and intrepid witnesses, established the convoluted chain of circumstantial evidence. Appeals were filed by the accused and cross appeals by the state for enhancement of the sentence.

This case is treated as a landmark for its exposition on circumstantial evidence as we all still seem to rely heavily on direct eyewitness accounts and motive. It was a complex conspiracy with myriad actors. Interestingly, all were convicted; the doers and the bystanders. This trial is also historic for the stand the defence lawyers took in admitting the affair. It is rare for defence lawyers to admit anything directly or indirectly incriminating.

The Motive

Mr A.N. Mulla, counsel for Chandresh, and Mr B.B. Lal, counsel for Dr Jain, correctly proceeded with the stratagem to not deny the affair between Dr Jain and Chandresh, the latter obtaining a decree of judicial separation from her husband and the flow of money by way of cheques and bank drafts from Dr Jain to Chandresh as proved by the prosecution. But motive to murder was denied. Counsel for Dr Jain contended, 'There was no earthly reason for Dr Jain to develop a devastating desire to marry Chandresh after their liaison had brought him all the desired gratification over so many years.' The contention was that Dr Jain had no motive whatsoever for having Vidya Jain killed.

Mr Mulla urged with equal vehemence that Chandresh also lacked motive to murder Vidya Jain and submitted that Vidya Jain's resentment and opposition to the intimacy between Dr Jain and Chandresh began as far back as April 1967, but Chandresh never did anything to harm Vidya Jain by way of retaliation or revenge. He contended, 'Nothing new having occurred to aggravate the hostility on Chandresh's part [if any], there could be no "compelling motive" for her to get Vidya Jain slain.'

The Delhi High Court observed:

'It is now well-settled that where direct evidence of commission of the crime is creditable, motive recedes into the background and is not accorded much importance. However, in a case depending wholly on circumstantial evidence motive is one of the material factors calling for consideration.

Not that an accused can be convicted merely on the proof of motive, but it certainly helps in the appreciation of the evidence bearing on the offence charged. Now, it may be possible to prove motive in one case while in another case no evidence thereof may be forthcoming. Its remaining shrouded in mystery would not, however, necessarily mean positive absence of motive. It is again beyond the pale of controversy that the prosecution need not make out adequacy of motive. How different persons behave in and react to diverse circumstances is incapable of prediction. What may appear to one as a very minor matter, to another may strike as grave enough for committing the most heinous crime. It would thus suffice for the prosecution to lead evidence suggesting a motive and leave the matter at that.

The Delhi High Court did find any motive in the love affair and the disproportionate payments, observing:

> It cannot be gainsaid that there was a motive for both Dr Jain and Chandresh to get rid of Vidya Jain. The affair between Dr Jain and Chandresh was neither ephemeral nor shallow. It was quite abiding and deep. Vidya Jain complained to her next-door neighbour, Mrs. Sheela Khanna (Public Witness 4), that Chandresh 'behaved on the dining table as if she was the mistress of the house'. Though Dr Jain terminated Chandresh's services as his Secretary within a month, it was only to buy peace in the house. The affair continued and the infatuation prospered. He continued remitting moneys to Chandresh regularly and the amounts involved were always in multiples of hundred and much more than Rs 300 the salary of which she had been deprived by her dismissal. It may be repeated that the one cheque he gave her on November 25, 1968 was for no less than Rs 8,400 the sum which she would have earned through 28 months' continuous labour.

Conspiracy

Conspiracy comes into being the moment the agreement to commit the crucial act is reached, and it does not cease to exist so long as the intention of acting upon the agreements exists.

When Rakesh and Chandresh went to hire Karan Singh as an assassin, the criminal conspiracy had come into existence. This conspiracy cannot be said to have come to an end when Karan Singh refused to carry out the part assigned to him (a conspiracy can be said to have ceased to exist only when either the objective of the conspiracy has been carried out or it is frustrated or aborted). Neither was the result achieved when Karan Singh refused to assassinate Vidya Jain. When Rakesh approached another person, Ram Kishan, and tried to enlist his services for killing Vidya Jain, it did not count as a new conspiracy but the same one. The same principle applies when the new assassins, Ujagar and Kartar, were engaged and the assignment was carried out successfully. '[T]he established facts on the record are that all along there was one conspiracy in operation, to kill Vidya Jain, and it continued right till the tragic demise of that unfortunate woman . . .' The charges framed against the appellants do not refer to three separate conspiracies, nor did the trial involve three conspiracies lumped together as suggested by the lawyers for the accused persons.

Who Should Be Hanged

There was a faint attempt to draw a distinction between Kartar and Ujagar since it was Ujagar who had settled the 'fees' for the crime and it was he who had inflicted the fatal blows, while Kartar had only held the victim down.

The Delhi High Court called it 'a distinction without a difference'. The high court observed:

> [T]he circumstances demonstrate that the murder could not be committed by one of them alone. In order to ensure that Vidya Jain should die positively without involving the slightest risk of apprehension for the assassins it was necessary to pin her down and render her incapable of shouting or shrieking for succour. This end could be achieved only if someone held her steady for well-aimed blows as well as sealed her mouth to stifle her cries. Kartar rendered that indispensable service and enacted a part no less potent than that of the man who wielded the knife. Kartar had equipped himself, moreover, with a .303 bore pistol and adequate ammunition had furnished a guarantee to Ujagar that nobody would impede his execution of the murderous design or endanger their easy access to the getaway car. He did not use his weapon since no necessity arose therefore In our opinion the extreme penalty of law is equally deserved by Ujagar and Kartar.

Dubious Distinction

Back when the crime was committed, it was more likely that the poor went to the gallows and the affluent survived, albeit in jails. On awarding the death penalty to the remaining co-accused, the bench ruled in the negative. Though Dr Jain, Chandresh and Rakesh were present at the time of the incident, and it is also true that they were active members of the conspiracy, the court chose to make a distinction and held that the crimes committed by the other co-accused would seem to stand at a lower plane as compared to the roles attributed to Ujagar and Kartar. 'They wished Vidya Jain dead and plotted her murder but all what they did would have accomplished nothing if Ujagar and Kartar had not undertaken to fulfil their wish and kill her.'

This decision seemed rather questionable since all had plotted and conspired to kill. It goes against the general law of the land that every conspirator who conspired to commit the act is equally guilty even if he or she did not commit the act. But Jain and Chandresh got off with life imprisonment. Ujagar and Kartar's sentence was enhanced from life imprisonment to death.

The Supreme Court expressed its anguish in these terms:

It is time that it was realised that the jurisdiction of this Court to grant special leave to appeal can be invoked in very exceptional circumstances. A question of law of general public importance or a decision which shocks the conscience of the Court are some of the prime requisites for the grant of special leave. If there is anything at all in this case which shocks our conscience it is this: that, if the death sentence was at all to be awarded, it should have been awarded to the hirelings and that the husband and his mistress who promised to pay to the hirelings large sums of moneys in order to procure the murder of the wife should have been awarded the lesser sentence.

Jain was sentenced to life imprisonment but let off after eleven years for good behaviour, while the hired assassins, Kartar Singh and Ujagar Singh, were hanged to death.

2

WOMEN WHO KILL

Introduction

The idea that women, who are usually only regarded as caregivers and nurturers, can kill in cold blood is difficult to accept in Indian society. Despite the belief that murders are mostly male-perpetrated, women are often also culprits, killing with the same heartlessness as a male killer. As is the case with other aspects of life, it is often seen that the motivations of women killers are different from their male peers. While a large number of male criminals are driven by sadism, sex, violence and lust, women's motivations are found to be mostly economic in nature. Motives that are common to both genders are greed and mental imbalance.

Time and again we come across crimes so heinous that it is difficult for the public to believe that women, who we often wrongly embody as only mothers, sisters or wives, i.e., mostly in compassionate, caregiving roles, can be a part of them. Of course, the truth is that gender has nothing to do with a person's ability to commit crimes.

According to the cases that have presented themselves, women usually target people whom they know or who are primary caregivers too. Statistics the world over show that women mostly kill people they are close to, or will first get close to people and then kill them. Their crimes are also more carefully thought out and planned meticulously, which is why it becomes possible to often escape with less punishment by the judiciary.

Renuka Shinde and Seema Gavit: Child Killers

Living in a civilized society, it is hard to digest the idea that a mother and the first teacher of her child would instruct her children in the horrific art of murder. In Maharashtra, a woman named Anjanabai, the matriarch of her family, taught and encouraged her family to murder and abuse young children for money. The entire episode came to light when her two daughters, twenty-nine-year-old Renuka Kiran Shinde, twenty-five-year-old Seema Mohan Gavit along with Renuka's husband, Kiran Shinde, were arrested in 1996. The three, along with Anjanabai, were accused of abducting and killing children, particularly those less than five years of age. Although they were accused of abducting thirteen children between 1990–96, and killing nine of them, they were eventually charged with only five murders.

The accused had been involved in petty theft for most of their lives. The idea to kidnap children came to them one day when Renuka was in a temple and trying to steal something. On being caught, she grabbed hold of her young son, who had accompanied her, and appealed to the crowd, asking them how a woman with a child could commit theft. The doubt she created was enough for the people to let her go. She realized that if she was accompanied by a child while committing her crimes, the likelihood of getting caught reduced significantly. She passed on the knowledge to her family, setting in motion the horrific crimes.

The matriarch of the family, Anjanabai, perfected the art of kidnapping for ransom, often instructing her daughters to grab a child from a crowded place, where it was not easy to look for a missing child. They would look for places where festivals were being celebrated or marketplaces where children tended to wander, and easily abduct their target. In this manner, they managed to kidnap children from many major cities in Maharashtra. They would keep these children in Pune at their residence.

The modus operandi of the sisters was easy: they would keep the child with them, often preferring to physically carry them while they went about their business of snatching purses and petty thievery. The children were promptly murdered when they attracted any attention or cried, or became too old to be carried in their arms.

The murders were committed in a manner that belies belief. Online news reports[1] detail that the murders were often committed by the sisters hurling the children on the ground with force, severely injuring them; the mother,

Anjanabai, would later finish the job introducing further trauma.

The murder of one of the kidnapped children called Santosh was carried out when he started crying. The two sisters banged the child's head on the floor and then their mother smashed the severely injured child against an iron pole till he died. His body was thrown under an autorickshaw. He was just eighteen months old.

Another eighteen-month-old girl child was gagged and dumped in a ladies' toilet in a handbag. Yet another was hung upside down from the ceiling and his head was repeatedly banged on the walls to punish him for talking to passers-by about his real parents. It's hard to imagine the extent of cruelty and greed of these women who went to the lengths of killing a two-year-old child by starving and beating him because he used to cry for his mother. However, this is also what helped cement every court's decision to award the perpetrators the most severe punishment.

After analysing the evidence and the prosecution witnesses, the Supreme Court, while confirming the death penalty stated:

> The appellants have been awarded capital punishment for committing these murders and their sentence was confirmed by the High Court. Going by the details of the case, we find no mitigating circumstances in favour of the appellant[s], except for the fact that they are women. Further, the nature of the crime and the systematic way in which each child was kidnapped

and killed amply demonstrates the depravity of the mind of the appellants. These appellants indulged in criminal activities for a very long period and continued it till they were caught by the police. They very cleverly executed their plans of kidnapping the children and the moment they were no longer useful, they killed them and threw the dead body at some deserted place. The appellants had been a menace to the society and the people in the locality were completely horrified and they could not send their children even to schools. The appellants had not been committing these crimes under any compulsion but they took it very casually and killed all these children, least bothering about their lives or agony of their parents.

We have carefully considered all aspects of the case and are also alive to the new trends in the sentencing system in criminology. We do not think that these appellants are likely to be reformed. We confirm the conviction and also the death penalty imposed on them. The stay of execution of the capital punishment imposed on these appellants shall stand vacated and the authorities are directed to take such further steps as are necessary to carry out the execution of capital punishment imposed on these appellants.

The case clearly revealed the extent of depravity of human beings and how both men and women are capable of committing horrific crimes when greed takes over. What hits us hardest is the realization that these chilling scenarios took place behind a mask of absolute ordinariness. Cruelty in its worst form was conspicuous in its banality, enhancing the fear it instils in our hearts. These women could be around us. Maybe we saw them and never noticed, but their crimes have shaken us to the core and have made them the first women to have received the death penalty since Independence.

The two sisters are now set to be the first women to be executed by hanging. They are currently awaiting their execution at Yerwada Central Jail in Pune. Their mother and matriarch of the family passed away in custody while awaiting trial in 1997. Renuka Shinde's husband, Kiran Shinde, received immunity for his testimony. The mercy petitions of the sisters were rejected by the President on 31 July 2014.

The Neeraj Grover Murder: A Murder Most Gruesome

The case of a media executive chopped into pieces and murdered became a matter of public obsession in 2008. A young couple was caught in flagrante delicto by the woman's boyfriend, which became the motivation for the crime. The people of India were so seized by the entire incident that a feature film was also made. The whole incident begs an oft-asked question: What is it about the human psyche that promotes and condones the killing of another human being in such a gruesome, unrelenting and unrepentant manner? Have we as a society failed to instil compassion in our generations?

Another question was also asked, albeit in smaller, closed circles: Did the media have the right to so conveniently demonize the accused without going through the process of law?

We have often seen crime generate interest. Gruesome, unimaginable crime more so, but does the media have any right to declare an accused guilty for a case that is sub judice? Does it not affect the psyche of the judicial process or of the judge, who is eventually a part of the society?

Neeraj Grover was a media executive. Maria Monica Susairaj was a Kannada actress who wanted to work in the TV industry. When she moved to Mumbai, Maria befriended Grover and they soon entered into an intimate relationship. However, Maria started having doubts about whether Grover was serious in aiding her career. The prosecution alleged that the plan to kill Grover was hatched on 6 May 2008, when Maria contacted Emile Jerome Joseph, her fiancé.

On 7 May 2008, Joseph went to Maria's apartment at around 7.30 a.m. Both the accused killed Grover. After the murder, Maria destroyed the evidence by chopping up the body and stuffing the parts into plastic bags along with other clothes and mattresses that had bloodstains on them. She took a car to the outskirts of Mumbai, to a place called Manor and purchased petrol to burn the bags and the evidence. She also got the walls of the apartment painted to hide the bloodstains.

On not receiving calls from her son, the mother of the victim contacted Neeraj's cousin, who approached Neeraj's friends as well as Maria. They later went to the Malad police station to record a missing persons report. The father of the victim approached the joint commissioner to initiate parallel proceedings for kidnapping, which was recorded on 20 May 2008.

The police interrogated Maria on 21 May, wherein she confessed to her and her fiancé's involvement in the murder of the victim. However, the statement was later retracted. She also took the police to the site where she had burnt the evidence. The police recovered a burnt skeleton as well as some other items, such as a bead necklace, a partly burnt deodorant bottle and a tin can. Bloodstains were also discovered at Maria's house. Joseph also agreed to show the police the location of the machine that was used to chop the body and the car used to transport it.

The court delved into whether the retracted confessional statement of Maria could be considered and stated:

> Taking into consideration the ratio laid down by Privy Council, and which is being followed by Apex court, I think aid of confessional statement can be taken in this case for certification or for lending the assurance to the guilt of the accused. I have gone through confessional statement of accused No. 1 carefully. The confessional statement goes to corroborate the circumstances, which have been brought on record to connect the accused No. 1 with killing of Neeraj Grover.
>
> [S]o the proved incriminating fact and circumstances, taken cumulatively, should form a chain so complete that there is no escape from the conclusion that within all human probability the accused No. 2 killed Neeraj Grover. The incriminating circumstances are incapable of explanation of any

other hypothesis than that of guilt of accused No. 2. Further part of confessional statement is about causing disappearance of evidence of killing Neeraj Grover. The circumstances, which have been brought on record through Satish Singh (P.W. 10), Vinod Mishra (P.W. 13), Dhiraj Shukla (P.W. 15), Vivek Tiwari (P.W. 19), Vaishali More (P.W. 20), Amarbahadur Yadav (P.W. 22) also go to connect the accused Nos. 1 and 2 for causing disappearance of evidence of killing Neeraj by screening themselves from legal punishment, which is also certified by the confessional statement of the accused No. 1. Therefore, I have no hesitation to hold that accused Nos. 1 and 2 with the intention to causing disappearance of the evidence of killing Neeraj Grover, attempted to destroy the evidence of killing of Neeraj Grover.

Therefore, according to the court's analysis of Maria's confession, it was concluded that only Joseph was responsible for the murder of the victim. In her statement she alleged that Joseph killed Grover, and raped and threatened to kill her too. When the court examined her statement and corroborated it with the injuries she had received on her hand, it was concluded that she had tried to stop a fight that had ensued between the two men. The court also went into whether the murder was pre-planned or not, and concluded that it was a spur-of-the-moment reaction of a young man finding his fiancé with another man at odd hours. If the murder had been pre-planned, then there would have been meticulous planning and the other accessories purchased after the murder would have been purchased before. Moreover, there seemed to be no prior motive for the murder of the deceased. The court believed Maria's initial statement and decided that she had just been an accessory to the crime and had in fact tried to stop it from happening.

After considering the evidence, the court held the accused guilty of both causing disappearance and destruction of evidence. The prosecution proved that Joseph killed the victim but the defence pleaded the first exception to murder, i.e., culpable homicide due to grave and sudden provocation. The court ruled out premeditation on the part of Joseph and maintained that he was under provocation. Both of the accused were charged under Section 201 for causing the disappearance of evidence, with a maximum penalty of three years. Joseph was charged under Section 304(1) of the IPC for culpable homicide not amounting to murder and was given ten years' rigorous imprisonment as well as a fine for Rs 50,000. Maria was convicted under Section 201 of the IPC for destruction of evidence and was given three years' rigorous imprisonment and a fine for Rs 50,000. Joseph was also convicted under the same offence and given the same punishment, for which his sentence would run concurrently.

In India, the process of trial by media is very prevalent. Right from the first bits of information it can find on the crime, the media tries to create its own chain of events, and often ends up creating a sensationalized version of the event. This incarnation of the media as a public court has damaged the very essence of judicial process and the fair and impartial ideals it stands for. The manhunt created by the media not only influences the mind of the judiciary but also corrupts public perception with useless sensationalism and half-baked facts. This results not only in the unfair victimization of the accused by the society but also in the harassment of their family and friends.

In this case, the media demonized the accused without looking at the hard facts, and even after the courts released Maria Susairaj on the basis of the facts placed before it, the media did not stop its persecution. In some reports, she was deemed 'characterless' and labelled not worthy of being a woman. The actual chain of events reveal the story of a woman who got caught in the middle of a crime, tried to stop it, was brutalized and raped, and was then forcibly made to destroy the evidence, for which she was penalized.

The difference between an accused and a convict is lost on laymen, and the media creates a situation where an accused becomes a convict even before the conviction. The idea that there was a woman involved in the crime created a huge furore, probably worse than if it had only been men. A woman accused of chopping up a body into pieces fanned our mindsets to feverish proportions and the media lapped it all up. This is a classic case of a media witch-hunt, which we as a civilized and educated society should avoid.

Phoolan Devi: The Making of an Outlaw

I never intended to become this . . . I was just so angry. Rich men would beat me up for daring to raise my eyes . . . My father would weep over injustices but he was helpless . . . I don't consider myself a lawbreaker.

—Phoolan Devi

The life of the Bandit Queen of India, Phoolan Devi, has by now passed into folklore; she is often touted as a killer and a murderer, and remembered as one of the most notorious outlaws in India. Accused of crimes ranging from dacoity to murder, Phoolan herself believed that she was innocent and that all the crimes she had committed were justified. The question then arises in the minds of observers: Does a hard life full of poverty, class difference and subjugation give a woman the right to commit mass murder? Was society or the law so impotent that she had to take matters in her own hands and kill and loot as an act of rebellion against the atrocities meted out to her as a young girl?

Although there is no correct answer to this, maybe we can better understand if we examine the life of this ordinary girl who rose into notoriety and passed into urban legend. The life of rejection and condemnation that she experienced in her childhood and teenage years offers a perspective into why she turned into the 'Bandit Queen'— something she is remembered for even today.

Even as a young girl, Phoolan showed a streak of rebellion and gumption that she would later become notorious for. Born to a poor fishing family, Phoolan was married off at the age of eleven. Apart from the obvious problem of being a child-bride, the marriage proved to be hellish for the young girl as she was mercilessly beaten by her husband. Phoolan managed to escape from the torture thus inflicted on her by running away. However, being a mere child in the deep hinterlands of India, she soon found herself in trouble. Phoolan got embroiled in a land dispute and found herself behind bars for a short while. After she was released, she travelled to the small village of Bhemai in Uttar Pradesh. It was here that a gang of upper-caste men brutally gang-raped her.

Sadly, for women of the lower Mallah caste, such treatment is not unusual. Many victims tend to absorb the pain of such incidents and do not speak up. Phoolan, however, was driven to a murderous rage and refused to just meekly accept the atrocities meted out to her. She joined a gang of bandits and rose as their leader.

Soon after, this young girl travelled with her gang to the same village where she had been gang-raped. She lined up all her twenty-two perpetrators and shot them dead in broad daylight. It is a wonder how Phoolan Devi managed to commit this crime—not only because it was unusual for a so-called lower-caste person, or even a woman, to kill the ones who wronged her, but because it took place in the heart of Uttar Pradesh, a state deeply divided by caste and class. However, the question remains: Was murder the solution or an answer to how the world had treated her?

The massacre caused unprecedented public anger, particularly because the subversive idea of caste superiority had been threatened—by a woman no less. Phoolan went into hiding in the deep forests near the border between Uttar Pradesh and Madhya Pradesh.

Two years later, Phoolan surrendered herself as part of an amnesty deal with the authorities. She spent eleven years in Gwalior Central Jail, without trial, before finally being released on parole in 1994. Thereafter, in a move that shocked many people, the Samajwadi Party government in Uttar Pradesh withdrew all charges filed against Phoolan. She was then seen as a modern-day Robin Hood, a messiah who had stood up against the rigid caste system, a leader of the oppressed masses. She went on to become a member of Parliament under the aegis of the Samajwadi Party in the eleventh Lok Sabha. However, the case against four of Phoolan's gang members in the Bhemai massacre is still pending, more than thirty years after the act.

In a sad end to her story, Phoolan was assassinated in 2001 outside her residence in Delhi by a group of three men.

Phoolan Devi was a regular Indian girl from a casteist society who found herself on the wrong side of the law because of her refusal to suffer injustice silently. Her actions could be seen as wrong or unlawful but were undoubtedly an act of rebellion owing to the circumstances of her life. Women are generally seen in an extremely limiting light, as the caregivers of a community, the loving maternal figures who look after the children and hold the men of the community together. This is especially true in a patriarchal society like India where independent women are often seen as rebellious. In this context, Phoolan Devi's story is the complete antithesis of what a stereotypical Indian woman is supposed to be like. However, behind the popular acts of her rebellion was a woman hardened into violent action due to her situation in life.

Living a life of poverty in a remote corner of India, Phoolan Devi found herself destined to a life of servitude to her family, but she had the courage to desire something more from her life. The mental scarring a little girl would experience at first being married against her will and then being treated as a pariah by her own people is not easy to imagine. Naturally, she wanted to get away from this social exclusion and she found solace in the community offered to her by the gang of dacoits she joined.

Cyanide Mallika

In our quest to understand the motivations of serial killers, we cannot possibly ignore the motive of greed. K.D. Kempamma, India's first female serial killer, was one such person, motivated purely by greed and the desire for better material comfort.

Kempamma, a forty-five-year-old at the time of her arrest, was given the moniker 'Cyanide Mallika' as she killed multiple people in and around Bangalore in cold blood using potassium cyanide.

Mallika preyed on vulnerable women, souls seeking peace in the city's temples. Often, these women were childless or facing marital problems, and were deeply religious, looking towards the divine for help. In a cruel twist of fate, their deliverance came in the form of death, dealt by the hand of a kindly looking, middle-aged woman who promised them that she could give them what they sought; she would claim to be skilled in the art of performing pujas and that she could make possible the miracles these desperate women were hoping for. After gaining the victims' confidence, Mallika would ask them to come dressed in expensive clothes and jewellery for the alleged rituals. The victim would then be taken to a desolate spot near the temple. Once there, Mallika would start the puja; she would ask her victims to close their eyes, forcibly pushing cyanide powder mixed with either food or drink into their mouths. Mallika carried out several such cold-blooded murders over the course of nine years in temples across Bangalore.

When Mallika was finally nabbed at a bus stand, she was in possession of cash and jewellery taken from some of the deceased. She also admitted to being guilty when her plea was recorded.

Cyanide Mallika is still a mystery. While we often try to justify the cruel nature of crimes by looking into the past to find something that went woefully wrong during the killers' formative years, the early life of Cyanide Mallika provides no clues, as there is little or no information about that time. However, on a bare reading of the facts surrounding the murders, one would think that the motivation for her committing the crimes was nothing but money. She asked her victims to come dressed in their best clothes and jewellery, which she would pocket after killing them and fleeing the crime scene. Even the police stated in Mallika's trial that she had committed the murders for the purpose of robbery and had no psychopathic tendencies.

As a young girl, Mallika was married to a tailor of modest means, but a simple life was apparently not her cup of tea. Deeply ambitious, she craved the luxuries of money and in her own words wanted a 'better life and material wealth'.

Even if Mallika's motive for committing the murders might have been the lure of wealth, her genesis as a criminal may lie in the early part of her life. Prior to the killings, Mallika had a chit fund that failed after a short while, after which she left her family and worked several low-paying jobs as a domestic help and an assistant to a goldsmith. It was probably during this time that she realized that crime was a way into wealth. The economic difficulty of her situation might be construed to be a reason for her criminal acts.

Her last victim, Nagaveni, proved to be her undoing; the police went after the mysterious killer who was preying on women around temples, little realizing that that killer was a harmless-looking forty-five-year-old woman.

This case was in direct contrast to our traditional thinking that women resort to gruesome crimes only when forced to, or under extreme circumstances that deeply affected the psyche. These cases seem to defy the traditional gender roles and the way we perceive them. The idea that women can kill seems to be a difficult one to digest for our conscience, but a mere look at these instances proves the opposite.

3

A TWIST OF FATE: THE YOUNG ONES

One of the most infamous cases of offence against children is the Billa–Ranga case of the late 1970s.

The case involved the kidnapping, abduction, rape and murder of two siblings. The nation watched closely, with bated breath, how the events unfurled after the discovery of the two dead bodies. It touched the right chord in every person and there was a lot of interest in the case till the murderers were brought to book and hanged. In today's times, it is the Nithari killings and the Aarushi murder case that have resonated with the public in a similar way.

The Billa–Ranga Case[1]

There are several landmark cases that establish, modify or repeal certain legal provisions. However, some cases, especially criminal ones, become landmarks because they represent a watershed moment in the sociolegal realm. The combined effect of the public shock and outcry, media pressure and the diligent investigation, albeit belated, surrounding these heinous crimes targeting the weaker members of society are often what make a case stand out in public memory. The case of the kidnapping and murder of Geeta and Sanjay Chopra is one such example.

Fate was unkind to these teenagers. It was an unfortunate series of incidents that took them to the Delhi Ridge (a portion of scrubland in the city), which was the scene of the murder. Generally, crimes consist of specific targets, but this was not one of those cases. The murderers were looking to pounce on any unsuspecting victim.

The siblings were seventeen and fifteen years old when life was mercilessly snatched away from them. Geeta was a second-year student of Jesus & Mary College, while Sanjay was studying in the tenth standard of Modern School. They were teenagers, about to enter the prime of their lives.

This was one of the first cases in India that involved positive public intervention and was covered by the media right from the commission of offence till the sentence was delivered.

Cruel Fate

It all happened on 26 August 1978, an otherwise pleasant evening. Sanjay and Geeta left their residence at about 6.15 p.m. to take part in *Yuvvani*, an All India Radio (AIR) programme airing at 8 p.m. I can mentally trace their footsteps and imagine what they would have experienced had they actually made it to the show, as I used to regularly compère *Yuvvani* back in college. The children's father, navy captain Madan Mohan Chopra, was supposed to pick them up from the venue at about 9 p.m.

On the same day, Billa (given name, Jasbir Singh) and Ranga Khus (given name, Kuljeet Singh), two hardened criminals who had been released from Arthur Road Jail in Mumbai (then known as Bombay) some time earlier, were prowling around the city of Delhi in a stolen mustard-coloured Fiat, looking for unsuspecting victims. Their plan was to kidnap children and extort money from their parents. The sister–brother duo had decided to hitch-hike to their destination—a very normal thing to do at the time—and were waiting near the Dhaula Kuan Ridge to find some transport to the AIR building on Parliament Street. It was raining when a doctor passing by saw the two children. He offered them a ride till the Gole Dak Khana, a landmark close to their destination. The children boarded the doctor's car and got off safely at the pre-decided point. While they were waiting to find their way to the AIR building, Ranga and Billa chanced upon the two innocent children. They had been skulking around, looking for hapless victims, and offered to give the teenagers a ride.

Billa and Ranga had planned the abduction beforehand. They had tampered with the inside door handles of the car, so that once closed, they would not turn and the victims would be locked inside. Geeta and Sanjay, in their urgency to reach the radio station, boarded the car. However, they soon realized the nefarious intentions of Billa and Ranga and started struggling to get out. At around the same time, one Mr Bhagwan Dass was exiting Gurudwara Bangla Sahib, a stone's throw from Gole Dak Khana, and proceeding towards North Avenue, which led to Rashtrapati Bhawan. It was about 6.30 p.m. when he noticed Billa and Ranga's Fiat parked near the entry gate of the Yog Ashram near Gole Dak Khana. Dass heard some noises issuing from inside the car. He tried to inquire into the reason for the noise, and saw a boy and a girl seated at the back, quarrelling with two men sitting in the front. Dass tried to reach the car but it sped away in the direction of Willingdon Hospital (now known as Ram Manohar Lohia Hospital). Dass immediately called the police control room to report the incident, stating that he had heard a woman shouting '*Bachao! Bachao!* [Help! Help!]' from inside the Fiat. The call was recorded at 6.44 p.m., within minutes of the incident taking place.

As the car sped away, another concerned citizen, one Mr Inderjeet Singh, chased the car for some distance on his scooter after hearing the shrieks of a girl from within the car. But the Fiat pulled away and disappeared from his sight. He alerted the Rajinder Nagar police station at around 6.45 p.m. Despite two complaints, no action was taken by the police. Instead of registering the second complaint, the police cited technical difficulties: that the alleged offence was a non-cognizable offence (one where the police cannot act without a court order) and that the scene of the alleged crime was outside their territorial jurisdiction. To be exact, it was at 7.40 p.m. when the duty officer at the police station relayed Singh's report to the police control room. With this, the Rajinder Nagar police washed their hands of the case. Eventually, at around 10.40 p.m., the police registered a complaint due to multiple eyewitnesses coming forward to report what they saw. However, no action was taken for an entire hour after the complaint had been registered.

The children, in the meanwhile, were putting up a brave fight against the criminals. Billa and Ranga had by now realized that the father of the children was an ordinary government servant who would not be able to pay a fat ransom. As a result, at about 9.30 p.m., they killed Sanjay and Geeta in the Upper Ridge Road jungle, in a place between Buddha Jayanti Park and Shankar Road, near the Upper Ridge Road roundabout. It is worth wondering, had adequate search efforts been put into operation, it is a possibility the children may have been saved.

Meanwhile, in the evening, the Chopra household, in Officers Enclave, was buzzing with activity. It was a moment of pride. The children were going to be featured on All India Radio. It was matter of great pride for the family. As the clock struck eight, the scheduled broadcast time, Captain Chopra tuned into the radio station. However, to the Chopras' utter surprise, the female voice on the radio was not their daughter's but someone else's. The Chopras rationalized the situation by presuming that either the programme had changed or they had not tuned into the right station.

As planned, Captain Chopra left the house at about 8.45 p.m. to pick up the children. On reaching the AIR building, he discovered that they were not there. Upon inquiring, he found to his utter shock that the children had never reported for the show in the first place. He called home frantically to check whether the children had reached home. After learning that they hadn't, he instantly rushed back and started making anxious phone calls to friends and family to determine their whereabouts. Finding no answers, he went all over town looking for them. At about 10.15 p.m., Captain Chopra called the police control room and lodged a missing persons report. Chopra himself went looking for them at the Willingdon Hospital and various other places, including the Parliament Street police station. Disheartened, he lodged another report at the Dhaula Kuan police station. By then, the police had already started to look for Geeta and Sanjay.

On the same day at about 10.15 p.m., Billa and Ranga sought treatment at Willingdon Hospital for a head injury sustained by Billa; they used aliases. An X-ray was also taken to examine the extent and seriousness of the injury. After receiving a few stitches, Billa was allowed to leave.

Two days after the kidnapping, on 28 August 1978, one Dhani Ram came across two dead bodies, a girl's and a boy's, while grazing his cattle at the Ridge. This information was relayed to the Rajinder Nagar police station, which, in turn, sent a wireless message to the Delhi Cantonment police station. As the police suspected the bodies to be Geeta's and Sanjay's, their parents were summoned to identify the bodies, which they conclusively did, and the missing persons case officially became a murder case. An FIR was registered at the Rajinder Nagar police station.

The Chase

The tragic abduction and murder of the siblings was quickly picked up by the media and turned into front-page news. Specific details were published daily in the newspapers. Doubts and questions were being raised against the government, prompting government representatives to release statements promising prompt action for apprehending the perpetrators of the heinous crime. The police also came under pressure to perform. They began the murder investigation by examining the crime scene from where the bodies had been recovered. In the meantime, the bodies were sent for a post-mortem. The doctors opined that the wounds on the bodies of Geeta and Sanjay had possibly been caused by a kirpan (a short sword or knife with a curved blade, worn as one of the five distinguishing signs of the Sikh Khalsa) and that the time of death was about fifty-four to sixty hours before the time of discovery of the bodies. The extensive media coverage of the case led to many witnesses coming forward to record their statements. Among them was the doctor who had given the teens a lift from Dhaula Kuan to Gole Dak Khana.

The police started investigations on various lines. Subsequent police investigations revealed that Billa and Ranga could possibly be involved in the commission of the crime. After learning about their antecedents, the Bombay police were contacted and a manhunt was launched for their capture. However, in the absence of any solid leads, the duo continued to evade arrest.

A major breakthrough in the investigation came on 31 August 1978, when the residents of Majlis Park informed the police about an abandoned mustard-coloured Fiat they had spotted. The car matched the description given by the eyewitnesses. The police recovered fingerprints, blood and hair samples and fake licence plates from the car. The DNA examination of the blood and hair samples proved beyond doubt that this was indeed the car that had been used to abduct the unfortunate siblings. The police recovered evidence from the Fiat which later proved to be very useful in convicting the accused, along with the testimony of the witnesses.

On 8 September 1978, Lance Naiks Gurtej Singh and A.V. Shetty were travelling with other military personnel in the military compartment of the Kalka Mail. They found the activities of two civilians who had entered the military compartment near Agra suspicious. The Lance Naiks were soon able to identify the two men as Billa and Ranga, suspected to be involved in the abduction and murder of the sister–brother duo, thanks to the extensive media coverage. They tied up the two suspects with ropes and handed them over to the station house officer of the Delhi railway station police in the early hours of 9 September. A live .32-mm gun was recovered from Billa while a kirpan was seized from Ranga.

The Trial

The trial of Ranga and Billa became the cynosure of all eyes. During interrogation, Billa and Ranga described their plan of stealing a car from somewhere, offering a ride to some young children, kidnapping them and extorting ransom from their parents. In case of any unforeseen contingency, they had decided they would kill the children. The valour and courage of young Sanjay and Geeta, who staunchly resisted surrender, as well as the fact that Billa and Ranga, while molesting the children, had managed to extract information about their father being a government servant who would be unable to pay a fat ransom, had angered the criminals and led to the children's murder.

At the trial, the prosecution presented a watertight case, with forensic evidence collected from various sites including the Ridge, the Fiat and many other places. In addition to such evidence and the confessional statements of both the accused, the prosecution submitted the testimonies of the various eyewitnesses. These Good Samaritans volunteered to testify against Billa and Ranga. This is in direct contrast to cases such as the Nirbhaya rape case, wherein people turned a blind eye to the occurrence of a crime to avoid being harassed by the police or other authorities. The eyewitnesses gave several accounts of the happenings of the fateful day of the children's disappearance and eventual murder.

The police, on the other hand, had made a major blunder by releasing to the press the photographs of the accused without having sufficient proof of their involvement in the crime. This led to the obvious defence that the witnesses who testified were preconditioned by the photographs published prominently across the national media, thus raising doubts about the identification process. Similarly, the tangibly hostile public sentiment towards Billa and Ranga, aroused by the excessive publicity given to the case by the national newspapers, was contended to be damaging to the prosecution's case.

Upon his arrest, Billa made a disclosure statement and was taken to the Willingdon Hospital for a medical examination. The doctor found a wound on his forehead and, upon examination, it was discovered that the X-rays of Billa's skull tallied with those of the man who had visited the hospital on the night of the murder. This established the presence of Billa and Ranga near the crime scene on 26 August 1978. The fingerprints on the X-ray slip, which were taken on the night of the incident, when the accused went to the hospital, were also proved to be Billa's.

Billa made another statement disclosing the whereabouts of the shop from which they had bought the kirpan used in the crime. Subsequently, they were produced before the metropolitan magistrate to record their fingerprints, and so on.

The post-mortem revealed that the wounds on the bodies were possibly caused by the kirpan and that Geeta had also been raped before being murdered. This discovery further enraged the public.

Kuljeet Singh, alias Ranga Khus, and Jasbir Singh, alias Billa, were convicted by the learned additional sessions judge for various offences in connection with the murder of Geeta and Sanjay Chopra. The two accused were sentenced to death for the offence of murder under Section 302 read with Section 34 of the IPC, and to varying terms of imprisonment under Sections 363, 365, 366 and 376 read with Section 34 of the code.

Ranga made a confessional statement in September 1978, but later retracted it in November. In October 1978 Billa also made a voluntary confessional statement but he too retracted the statement a month later. In their confessional statements, both of them testified against one another. This is a classic case of prisoner's dilemma, where one prisoner does not know what the other prisoner is going to say, and, consequently, because of mutual distrust, both end up testifying against each other.

The trial court noted that:

> Evidence produced by the prosecution, as already discussed, leaves no doubt that the appellants were seen at about 6.40 p.m. with the deceased in the Fiat car at Gole Dak Khana and later on the road leading to Shankar Road, at about 7.30 P.M. they were with the deceased at Buddha Jayanti Park; the deceased breathed their last at about 9.30 P.M., and the appellants came to Willingdon Hospital at 10.15 P.M. The appellants give no explanation as to what did they do to Sanjay and Geeta. On the other hand, they have given false explanations. The circumstantial evidence leaves no room for doubt that the appellants are the murderers.

The order of conviction and sentence, including the sentence of death, was confirmed by the Delhi High Court by a judgment on 16 November 1979.

The high court while agreeing with the trial court's verdict, made the following observations:

We are satisfied that the appellants are desperadoes who have no compunction in killing.

They hit upon a most diabolical plan of a cold-blooded, ruthless, cruel murder of two young innocent teenagers.

Immediately after killing Sanjay, the appellants had no compunction in raping Sanjay's helpless sister by stripping her naked. After satisfying their beastly lust, they killed her and threw her body in the bushes. Evidently the appellants had a fiendish sadistic pleasure in committing the crime.

Whether we look at the crime or at the criminals the conclusion is irresistible that with the elimination of the appellants the society would be much better off and its safety will no longer be endangered. Indeed, to award any other sentence except death sentence will amount to complete failure of justice. We are in complete agreement with the special reasons given by the trial judge for awarding the death sentence.

The Supreme Court of India dismissed the appeals against the conviction and upheld the verdict of the high court.

Post-Trial Consequences

As is common practice in India, even after confirmation of the sentence by the highest court of the land, the petitioners still find grounds for yet another appeal to the Supreme Court. After the dismissal of the special leave petitions, Ranga filed a writ petition,[2] praying for reconsideration of the death-sentence penalty on the grounds that it was Billa who was the main perpetrator of the crime and not him, which was dismissed by the Supreme Court.

The Supreme Court held that: '[The duo] sail on the same boat and must stand or fall together . . . The survival of an orderly society demands the extinction of the life of persons like Ranga and Billa who are a menace to social order and security. They are professional murderers and deserve no sympathy even in terms of the evolving standards of decency of a maturing society.'

Yet another petition[3] was filed before the Supreme Court that raised the contention that the court should scrutinize the denial of clemency by the President of India. Billa and Ranga submitted that by refusing to commute the death sentence imposed upon the petitioner into a lesser sentence, the President had transgressed his discretionary power under Article 72 of the Constitution. The Supreme Court noted that this particular provision is one that enjoins in itself a duty to exercise the clemency power fairly and reasonably. The court, however, refused to go into the scope of the powers of the President and any guidelines for the exercise of power under Article 72 as such exercise of power has to be determined on a case-by-case basis. In this instance, the only sentence possible was that of the death penalty. The verdict was unyielding—the convicts were professional killers and deserved no mercy.

Before the execution of the sentence, however, yet another petition was made before the Supreme Court. This new petition was different from some of the others filed in connection to the case. Ms Prabha Dutt, a reporter for the *Hindustan Times*, sought the issuance of a writ of mandamus (meaning a writ that is 'issued as a command to an inferior court') directing the Delhi administration and the superintendent of Tihar Jail to allow her to interview Billa and Ranga. Under the rules of the jail manual, only the relatives, friends and legal advisers can be allowed to meet the death-row convicts. The Supreme Court, in a landmark decision in *Prabha Dutt v. Union of India* in 1981,[4] ruled that if the convicts were willing to give the interview then there was no reason for denying the interview.

Bravery and Valour

History will record the bravery and courage of these children who fought against all odds. One of the witnesses stated that he had seen the girl catching hold of the driver sitting in front of her and raising an alarm, while the boy quarrelled with the person sitting next to the driver. The Indian government bestowed the Kirti Chakra gallantry award on Geeta and Sanjay Chopra on 5 April 1981. In 1978, the Indian Council for Child Welfare instituted two annual bravery awards for children under the age of sixteen, the Sanjay Chopra Award and the Geeta Chopra Award, given each year along with the National Bravery Award.

The murder of children is always particularly devastating. This case is especially heart-rending as the victims were siblings and the family lost two of their children to the same atrocious crime, on the same day. The grief and anger of the parents in such cases is unimaginable and unfathomable. The case touched a chord with every Indian and generated a huge public outcry. It is this general uproar that led to vigilant pursuit by the police and the eventual apprehension of the criminals. However, the Delhi High Court castigated the police, saying: 'Before parting with this case we are constrained to observe that the lives of the two children could have been saved if the police had acted promptly . . . Had flying-squad cars been put into operation immediately, there was a good chance for preventing the murders. A general alarm should have been sounded to apprehend the culprits.'

We can't turn the clock back. But we have lessons to learn. We can only hope that the next time there is a complaint, it should not fall on deaf ears. Promptness and diligence by the police is needed not only after the offence but also for crime prevention. I end this chapter by saying that full accountability on the part of the authorities must be ensured so that next time a Sanjay and a Geeta may be saved.

4

BLOODLESS MURDER: DEFAMATION

The subcontinent of India takes pride in its democracy. It is often a wonder that a nation as vast and diverse as ours has had a successful democratic government for seventy years now. It often strikes me that the cornerstone of a true democracy is always the degree of freedom of speech and expression afforded to its people. The idea that the citizens of a country can express themselves without any fear of unjust retribution has always played an important part in the functioning of global affairs. I am of the firm belief that the reason India stands as one of the foremost functioning democracies is that our freedom to speech and expression is uncompromisingly protected.

Free speech and expression, though rightly irrefutable, can often take the turn into the territory of defamation if not used responsibly. Statements made wantonly, without confirming facts, have the potential to harm beyond reparation.

In the case of *Vishwanath Agrawal v. Sarla Vishwanath*,[1] the Supreme Court observed: 'Reputation is not only the salt of life but also a revenue generator for the present as well as posterity.' In *Umesh Kumar v. State of Andhra Pradesh*,[2] the court observed that the personal rights of a human being include the right of reputation. A good reputation is an element of personal security and is protected by the Constitution equally along with the right to enjoyment of life, liberty and property, and as such it has been held to be a necessary element with regard to the right to life of a citizen under Article 21 of the Constitution.

When we look at the law of defamation, the first question that strikes us is the concept of 'reputation'. What exactly constitutes reputation? Is it goodwill? Is it the status one has in the eyes of society? Or is it the character we associate ourselves with? Reputation can loosely be understood as property, albeit intangible, and is often associated with the status or character we seem to possess in the society we live in.

In India, particularly, reputation is considered to be a huge asset. Indian history is rife with examples of men who rose to hero status trying to protect their honour, or of women who are revered as goddesses because they died trying to protect their reputations. In almost all societies, reputation is the gauge by which the social worth of an individual is assessed.

Just like the idea of good and evil, nature seems to exist in opposites, so the idea of reputation coexists with notoriety. The law of defamation seeks to curb that. It exists to protect citizens and organizations from notoriety and seeks to curb loose tongues and rogue ink to mar the reputation painstakingly created by people so that no damage is done by wanton minds and wagging tongues.

The origin of defamation can be traced to the idea of *scandalum magnatum*—'the slander of great men'—a concept invoked to protect the carefully built and nurtured reputations of aristocrats. The IPC, however, derives the law of defamation from more humble backgrounds, which many argue was a direct result of the need to protect the interests of the British Raj in colonial India. The legislature, however, has, in its wisdom, retained these statutes in the IPC under Sections 499 and 500.

Section 499 states:

> Defamation: Whoever, by words either spoken or intended to be read, or by signs or by visible representations, makes or publishes any imputation concerning any person intending to harm, or knowing or having reason to believe that such imputation will harm, the reputation of such person, is said, except in the case hereinafter expected to defame that person.

Section 500 states that whoever defames another shall be punished with simple imprisonment for a term which may extend to two years, or with a fine, or with both.

Reputation and defamation are at opposite ends of the same spectrum. The idea of repute as an intangible property creates a case for a strong and dynamic law. It is evident that there is a need to protect an individual from defamation, and the tort of defamation seeks to achieve that purpose.

The guiding rationale seems to have its roots in the age-old law enumerating that 'my right stops where the other's begins'. Various judgments of the Supreme Court have consistently held that no individual may act in a way to denigrate or subjugate another's right to reputation.

The law of defamation can be broadly seen under two heads. One, libel, which has a physical representation (in the form of pictures or writings) of the harm-causing content, making it permanent in nature. And, two, slander, which is mostly transient in character, and heard; in essence through spoken word or gestures.

In the Indian context, defamation is classified as either criminal or as a tort.

Under Section 499, the definition of defamation is subject to ten exceptions. Section 500 provides for imprisonment for up to two years for the offence. The offence is non-cognizable and bailable, and the accused can be taken into custody with only a warrant. Also, a complaint needs to be filed with the magistrate for action.

The Constitution of India has always aimed to protect and uphold human dignity. The right to reputation comes under the umbrella of rights guaranteed under the Constitution and acts as an enabler to other dignities promised under the law of the land.

Although touted as property, the right to dignity is not as simple as material possession; it encompasses social and territorial values and cannot just be weighed in monetary terms. It is often true that an injury to reputation is as painful, or even more, than actual physical injury. Unlike other crimes, insult or rumour does not leave traceable, tangible evidence behind, but it can cause as much—if not more—hurt than physical injury. In such circumstances, can decriminalization of the law of defamation be feasible? Is it possible to compensate injury and insult with money and be satisfied with it?

In India, defamation was an idea that was given legislative sanctity by Lord Macaulay in 1837. The law of defamation was initially created to protect the British Raj and its officers from harm. The offence of defamation was at that time a tool in the hands of the colonizers to aid and abet their interests. It was a net used to catch all activities by Indians that were not conducive to their own benefit. Meetings, pamphlets and activities that were suspected of being anti-British were all tried under the law and ruthlessly punished.

Despite having a less-than-noble beginning, the law of defamation was given a place in our newly free nation post independence. However, it gave rise to a new question: When the interests of the new republic were not in conflict with the interest of its citizens, did the law of defamation still require to be criminalized?

In India, defamation may have civil or criminal connotations, but the laws controlling it remain the same, regardless of the situation. The claimant is required to prove that a person's reputation has been injured by statements. Once it is proved that there was some damage to reputation, it lies with the defence to prove that the case is covered under one of the ten exceptions provided under Section 499.

The exceptions offered are wide, and protection is extended for instances involving true statements, public good and opinion in good faith. Despite these exceptions, it is prudent to keep in mind that the freedom of speech and expression protected under the Indian Constitution is subject to reasonable restriction, including protection from defamation.

International law recognizes defamation as a wrong towards the public at large. The Universal Declaration on Human Rights of 1948, under Article 12, clearly stipulates that no one shall be subjected to an attack on their honour and reputation.

The two cases we discuss here have defined the parameters of the law of defamation, exploring the right to free speech and expression, and the point at which it transverses reasonability and lands in the domain of criminality. The case of the south Indian actress Khushboo, emanating from a spurt of defamation cases, stands out as a milestone judgment on the freedom of speech, constitutionality versus constitutional morality, and a host of other directly and indirectly related issues.

Khushboo v. Kanniammal

In a country where people are frequently dumped into the criminal machinery for exercising their fundamental right to freedom of speech and expression, where people are condemned for speaking against the 'majoritarian belief' and where people are highly intolerant when it comes to morality, the case of *Khushboo v. Kanniammal*[3] stands out as an anomaly.

As a lawyer, I often wonder about the juxtaposition of criminal defamation and morality. I had the honour of representing the actress in this case and had the opportunity to study first-hand the matter in depth vis-à-vis what was known as part of the public perception. Morality is a subjective concept, and what is immoral may be perfectly moral for some other person or group. The perceived immorality by one dominant group cannot be labelled the norm for all or as an offence under the law.

Under Article 21, an adult woman has unrestricted liberty to marry anyone she likes and live with anyone she wants. The Supreme Court, in *Lata Singh v. State of UP & Anr*,[4] has held that a live-in relationship between two consenting adults does not amount to any offence. There exists a difference between the law and morality, and even if something is assumed to be immoral, it may still be legal.

The courts do not exist for moral policing or to impose moral standards upon people. It is up to the people themselves to choose whether they want to live with someone outside of wedlock or enter into a customary legal relationship of marriage. Cases such as *Shreya Singhal v. Union of India*[5] have held that laws must give a citizen 'fair warning', i.e., a reasonable person should know that a certain sort of conduct is prohibited. This argument is perfectly summed up by the former justice of the US Supreme Court Oliver Wendell Holmes in his seminal 1897 article, 'The Path of the Law': 'It is revolting to have no better reason for a rule of law than that so it was laid down in the time of Henry IV. It is still more revolting if the grounds upon which it was laid down have vanished long since, and the rule simply persists from the blind imitation of the past.'

The events that sparked off the case arose in September 2005, when *India Today* magazine conducted a survey on the sexual habits of people residing in the bigger cities of India. Premarital sex was one of the issues discussed, and views were gathered from the different segments of society. Khushboo, a south Indian actress, opined on the issue, saying that the incidence of premarital sex was an increasing phenomenon: 'According to me, sex is not only concerned with the body, but also concerned with the conscious . . . Our society should come out of the thinking that at the time of the marriage, the girls should be with virginity (sic) . . . But when having sexual relationship the girl should protect themselves (sic) from conceiving and getting venereal diseases.'

This statement was then covered by another Tamil daily magazine, *Dina Thanthi*, attracting several conversations on the matter. The actress vehemently defended herself by saying: 'The persons who are protesting against my interview are talking about which culture? Is there anyone who does not know about sex in Tamil Nadu? Is there anyone who does not know about AIDS? How many men and women do not have sex before marriage? Why are people saying that after the marriage the husband and wife should be honest and faithful to each other? One should have confidence in the other, only to avoid the mistakes from being committed. If the husband, without the knowledge of the wife, or the wife, without the knowledge of the husband, [either] have sex with other persons, if a disease is caused through that, the same will affect both the persons. It will also affect the children. Only because of this, they are saying like that (sic).'

The repercussions of this statement unravelled in the form of as many as twenty-one criminal complaints being filed against the actress under Sections 499, 500, 509, 153-A and 292 of the IPC, read with Sections 4 and 6 of the Indecent Representation of Women (Prohibition) Act, 1986, in various separate jurisdictions. The ignominy of the situation was that Khushboo was made to run from pillar to post in courts spread across several territories. To get respite from this constant prosecution, she approached the High Court of Madras to quash these complaints. Despite clear indications that this was a matter of political victimization, the high court refused to step in and directed the chief judicial magistrate to combine all the complaints.

The high court's judgment unfortunately is a reflection of the exact patriarchal bent of mind that large sections of society are today up in arms against. The court expounded on how the actress was educated only till class eight, that she did not have a world view except her knowledge of cinema and how she could in no way be an expert on sexology. It went on to state:

In India, chastity and love are explicitly regulated, that is why, women are assigned an elevated position in society and they are ordinarily not approachable by men except through legal means viz., marriage. In the other situation, where love and chastity are implicitly promoted; but not regulated, one could witness, women's position is subject to the utter tedium of placing themselves at the disposal and protection of their men. One may wonder as to which one of these two sets of conditions are apt to enhance love and chastity. Incidentally, it is notable that the so called open or permissive societies, blindly lauded by the petitioner, are ipso facto incapable of promoting conditions for any deep and intense love relationships. Their conditions lead to waywardness and wantonness, in the process of seeking transient affairs, if not while indulging in momentary and lustful pleasures.

Dating begins at a very young age and every socially well-adjusted youngster is expected to have several girlfriends and boyfriends by a certain age. Use of condoms by school going children has become a common phenomenon there. Thus, those who grow up in the West are weaned on sex in both subtle and not so subtle ways. That is why, to many Westerners, sex can be worthwhile as long as it embodies the sweetness mutually attainable by lovers. Individuals of opposite sex there prefer the desirability and enjoyability of living together in mutual love and comfort to the constant annoyance and boredom of living as singles. They aim at maximising enjoyment of life. In quite contrast thereto, in Indian society, sex is regarded as something inexorably desirable in itself only through marriage and one would pray while entering conjugal life that the marital relationship should continue even after death in the world of souls. If such social set-up strengthened by moral and ethical ideology is criticized, it would result in adverse impact both emotional and consequential.

After this, Khusboo and her lawyers approached me to move the Supreme Court. It is in rare cases that the apex court quashes complaints. After vociferous arguments, the court held that Khushboo's views and opinions did not qualify as defamatory under Section 499 of the IPC.

The entire furore is important to examine as it raises questions about our capacity to tolerate views that are not in consonance with those of the mainstream. A mere reference to the increasing incidence of premarital sex and the call for its societal acceptance was challenged on the grounds of it being beyond the protection of the freedom of speech and expression, in spite of it being defamatory in nature, interfering in the domain of personal autonomy and insulting the modesty of a woman or an identifiable group of women.

On observing the chronology of the case, one may infer that the whole controversy revolves around two debates, namely, the societal acceptance of premarital sex and the disproportionate response to the remarks.

In relation to the first point of debate on the societal acceptance of premarital sex, the Supreme Court, after deliberations, concluded that though it is true that a majoritarian view in our society restricts sexual contact between partners, there is no statutory authority that declares consensual sex (with the exception of adultery) to be an offence outside the marital setting. The court recognized that the substance of the controversy did not touch on the issue of whether premarital sex is socially acceptable or not. The real concern was the disproportionate response people had to the actress's remarks.

It was held that Khushboo neither intended to cause harm to the reputation of complainants, nor could any actual harm be discerned from her remarks. She had not suggested that all women in Tamil Nadu engage in premarital sex but had merely addressed how premarital sex was viewed in the society at the time.

The Khushboo judgment not only brings to light the totalitarian face of the majoritarian belief but preserves the confidence of rational people in the judiciary.

The judgment, rendered by Justice B.S. Chauhan, which upheld the sanctity of thoughts protected under Article 19(1)(a) of the Indian Constitution, states: 'Even though the constitutional freedom of speech and expression is not absolute and can be subjected to reasonable restrictions on grounds such as "decency and morality" . . . We must lay stress on the need to tolerate unpopular views in the sociocultural space . . . we must also promote a culture of open dialogue when it comes to societal attitudes.'

In this case, the court stated that no prima facie case could be drawn for any statutory offences asserted by the original complainants. With respect to the allegation of defamation charges, it was held that it was amply clear that the accused must intend to harm the reputation of a particular person, or should have reasonably known that his or her act would cause such harm. On analysing the facts, it was crystal clear that the actress did not intend any such thing to the reputation of the complainant and, thus, both mens rea and actus reas were missing.

The court also went on to state: 'It is difficult to fathom how the appellant's views can be construed as an attack on the reputation of anyone in particular. Even if we refer to the remarks published in *Dina Thanthi* . . . there is no direct attack on the reputation of anyone in particular . . . Even if we consider these remarks in their entirety, nowhere has it been suggested that all women in Tamil Nadu have engaged in premarital sex . . . It is a clear case of the complainants reading in too much into the appellant's remarks.'

The harassment to the actress was so clear that the Supreme Court went on to opine that the criminal complaints filed were mala fide in nature, and that in order to prevent the abuse of the criminal law machinery, magistrates, in the future, should use their statutory power to direct an investigation into the allegation before taking cognizance of the offence.

This case also launched an entire media debate on the morality of a live-in relationship. In a society like ours, the idea that live-in relationships existed was difficult to palate. Things went from bad to worse when a revered actress, in whose name temples had been built in the southern territories of India, voiced her stance openly and defended it too. I personally am not in favour of live-in relationships; I find them transient and unstable, but I did support

Khushboo's right to an idea and opinion. What she said was the truth and she had stated it, to the ire of many. It was also such an aberration because Khushboo herself is happily married with two children. It was heartening to see the Supreme Court leave behind patriarchal ideas and come to the rescue of free thought and ideas.

Interesting observations were made during the course of the arguments; the courts even went so far as to ask: 'Please tell us what is the offence and under which section. Living together is a right to life.'

It was also noticed by the court that most of the cases had been filed against the actress by members of a rival political party who had thus turned the whole debate into a morality–politics issue.

I have great respect for Khushboo, who stood by her words because she had the courage to face the reality and call a spade a spade.

Subramanian Swamy v. Union of India

From Khushboo's case, which was an example of vexatious litigation in the domain of the law of defamation, we traverse and come to the question: If the law has become an instrument of oppression and a tool to harass freethinkers, why does the Indian legislature continue to provide criminal genesis to it?

The answer to the question lies in the recent judgment of *Subramanian Swamy v. Union of India*,[6] where the Supreme Court looked extensively into the criminal nature of the law of defamation and why it continues to this day.

The petition challenged the constitutional validity of Sections 499 and 500 of the IPC as relevant, calling it a relic of the past and a symbol of the colonial era, which was holding freedom of speech and expression hostage to the threat of criminal prosecution.

The judgment began by discussing the idea of 'reputation'. Referencing several past judgments, it whittled down the definition of reputation to be:

[F]undamentally a glorious amalgam and unification of virtues which makes a man feel proud of his ancestry and satisfies him to bequeath it as a part of inheritance on posterity. It is a nobility in itself, for which a conscientious man would never barter it with all the tea of China or for that matter all the pearls of the sea. The said virtue has both horizontal and vertical qualities. When reputation is hurt, a man is half-dead. It is an honour which deserves to be equally preserved by the downtrodden and the privileged. The aroma of reputation is an excellence which cannot be allowed to be sullied with the passage of time. It is dear to life and on some occasions it is dearer than life. And that is why it has become an inseparable facet of Article 21 of the Constitution. No one would like to have his reputation dented, and it is perceived as an honour rather than popularity.

The court then proceeded to weigh the principle of reputation against the principles enumerated under the freedom of speech and expression, dividing the contention into four parts:

1. Defamation can only include a civil action but not a criminal action.

2. Even if defamation is considered to include in itself the criminal offence, it has to be understood in association with the phrase, 'incitement to an offence', where the principle of noscitur a sociis is required to be applied, which states that the meaning of an ambiguous word should be determined by considering the words with which it is associated in the context.

3. The intention of Article 19(2) of the Constitution is to deal within itself the public-law remedy but not to take in its ambit an actionable claim under the common law by an individual.

4. Since assault on an individual's reputation cannot be considered as a fundamental right, therefore, criminal defamation cannot claim to have its source in Article 19(2).

For the purpose of determining whether defamation is civil or criminal in nature, case laws were relied upon and it was found that defamation cannot be given a 'restrictive meaning'. The court was confronted with the question of whether the harm caused by defamation is restrictive to only individual or extends to the society as a whole. It stated:

> [I]ndividuals constitute the collective. Law is enacted to protect the societal interest. The law relating to defamation protects the reputation of each individual in the perception of the public at large. It matters to

an individual in the eyes of the society. Protection of individual right is imperative for social stability in a body polity and that is why the State makes laws relating to crimes. A crime affects the society. It causes harm and creates a dent in social harmony. When we talk of society, it is not an abstract idea or a thought in abstraction. There is a link and connect between individual rights and the society; and this connection gives rise to community interest at large. It is a concrete and visible phenomenon. Therefore, when harm is caused to an individual, the society as a whole is affected and the danger is perceived.

While analysing the concept of crime with reference to its effect on society at large, the court went on to state: '[T]reating defamation as a criminal offence can have no public interest and thereby it does not serve any social interest or collective value is sans substratum.'

It was urged that defamation has been described as an offence under Section 499 of the IPC, where it protects an individual's reputation in his or her own eyes, which is subjective, and therefore cannot be held to the level of public interest. Thus, in order to resolve the issue presented, the court was required to scrutinize whether the criminalization of defamation under Section 499 withstands the test of non-excessiveness, public interest and non-arbitrariness.

The Supreme Court answered the question, upholding the constitutional validity of the criminal character of the law of defamation, and stated: '[T]herefore, in the ultimate conclusion, we come to hold that applying the doctrine of balancing of fundamental rights, existence of defamation as a criminal offence is not beyond the boundary of Article 19(2) of the Constitution, especially when the word "defamation" has been used in the Constitution.'

The court concluded that keeping in mind the constitutional values and the government decision to not repeal the pre-constitutional defamation law, it is difficult to reach a final conclusion on whether the existence of criminal defamation is absolutely removed from the ambit of freedom of speech and expression, as echoed by the court. 'As a prescription, it neither invites the frown of any of the articles of the Constitution, nor can its very existence be regarded as an unreasonable restriction.'

On a detailed analysis of Section 499 of the IPC, the court concluded that neither the main provisions and explanations, nor the exception remotely indicate any vagueness.

An argument was also raised by the plaintiff where it was contended that Section 499 defeats the doctrine of proportionality. This was rejected by the court, which held that criminal defamation does not impede the doctrine and at the same time it also complies with the test of reasonableness.

I am of the personal opinion that the judgment, though subjected to criticism on various public platforms, has sound legal principles at its core. In a country where reputation is often considered more valuable than life, the decriminalization of defamation would dilute the seriousness of the harm it has the ability to cause. At the base of this lies the idea that honour cannot be recompensed monetarily and that is a collective thought of the majority of the society. The legislature has exercised its wisdom to uphold this idea by retaining defamation as a crime.

It is, however, of absolute importance that the freedom of speech and expression be exercised in a positive manner. The reasonable restrictions envisaged make sure that this vital liberty given to the citizens of India is not misused and does not become a tool for harassment and vendetta.

5

CIVIL SOCIETY: A CHAMPION OF JUSTICE

PRIYADARSHINI MATTOO AND JESSICA LAL

When I think about the profession I have dedicated my life to, I realize that the essence of law is the codification of societal norms. We can see this especially in India, where, till now, a uniform civil code has not been made applicable. We, as a society, are so diverse and varied, but there are a few common, basic features that characterize us as civilized human beings. There are some nodal points in our collective consciousness, which, if provoked, will invariably lead to mass public outrage, despite restrictions placed on us by class, caste or religion.

So what propels this mass uprising? When does human outrage take over from our nurturing prejudices and we, collectively, as humans, bay for blood, forcing the system to take stock?

Instances of public outrage are as old as society itself—when Marie Antoinette asked the peasants to eat cake, or, as seen in the present times, when a young girl was brutally murdered in a bus roaming the streets of Delhi. In our nation, too, the rage of civil society has existed since the birth of modern India. I would go so far as to say that the birth of modern India itself was a result of outrage on the part of the civil society against the British oppression.

We feel proud when we bring change as a society— we fight for what is right and force the system to change. Often, the incidents that jerk us awake are horrific and brutal, but they bring about change, and for me, a sense of pride in our ability to recognize and take action against atrocities. Throughout my career I have been fortunate enough to be a witness to and be a part of these civil-society awakenings, two of which involved Priyadarshini Mattoo and Jessica Lal.

The murders of Priyadarshini Mattoo and Jessica Lal shocked the public conscience, particularly because the two women embodied the better aspects of modern India. They were both educated and were looking forward to successful careers in their chosen fields. Priyadarshini, a student at Delhi's premier law college, was the ideal daughter any parent would wish for. Jessica symbolized the aspirations of the Indian youth as a successful model enjoying her life in the nation's capital. The murders of these respectable, successful citizens of society struck a chord with the public.

The public authorities, in both cases, failed to do their duty in the pursuit of justice. Priyadarshini's killer was acquitted by the trial judge even though the chain of circumstances was complete and consistent with the guilt of the accused. In Jessica's case, the police watched as the murderer bribed and intimidated his way to freedom.

Where public authorities failed, civil society succeeded. The media and the public played a pivotal role in ensuring the murderers received fitting punishment. Demonstrations were held in Delhi demanding justice for these young victims. The media covered the trials in minute detail, forcing the system to take prompt notice of the cases. The cases were heard on a day-to-day basis by the Delhi High Court, and the social uproar they created led to justice in both instances, despite the influence purportedly exerted by the accused. The killers of Priyadarshini Mattoo and Jessica Lal are now serving life-imprisonment terms for their heinous crimes.

The two cases marked a new epoch in the lethargic legal system and gave many victims the assurance that they are not at the mercy of the system. Civil society can often make a mark, but usually, a 'media trial' is regarded negatively in criminal jurisprudence. Fortunately, despite the abject failure of the investigative agencies, there was enough compelling evidence in these two cases. It was the mindset that needed a push.

This chapter aims to analyse the role of social pressure in bringing these cases to justice. The two cases of Priyadarshini Mattoo and Jessica Lal present the most potent examples of the power of civil society.

Priyadarshini Mattoo

Serious questions are raised when a judge states a man is guilty, yet declines to convict him. After all, why would a judge refuse to punish a man he proclaims to be guilty? As baffling as it might sound, this is exactly what the trial court judge did in Priyadarshini Mattoo's case. In a judgment that shocked the nation, the judge apologetically held: 'I know that he is the man who committed the crime. [But] I acquit him, giving him the benefit of doubt.'

One of the famous tenets of criminal jurisprudence as stated by Voltaire in 1749, ''tis much more Prudence to acquit two Persons, tho' actually guilty, than to pass Sentence of Condemnation on one that is virtuous and innocent.' Or as echoed by Benjamin Franklin, 'It is better 100 guilty Persons should escape than that one innocent Person should suffer.' But letting the guilty escape is not doing justice either. In this case, the man was not innocent by any stretch of imagination, as shown by the evidence produced at the trial. So then why was he acquitted? The answer lies in Priyadarshini Mattoo's murder trial.

The harassment of Mattoo started in a manner that has been glorified by Bollywood—boy follows girl, constantly telling her he loves her and tries to convince her to go out with him. Unfortunately, in this case, stalking led to the downfall of two young lives. Mattoo was a twenty-five-year-old student at Delhi University's prestigious Faculty of Law, and Santosh Singh was her senior. Santosh had feelings for Priyadarshini and used to follow her around everywhere, almost stalking her, even after she graduated from the university. Santosh harassed and intimidated Priyadarshini on numerous occasions. Increasingly frustrated by his behaviour, she filed a police complaint against him as a last recourse. The police summoned Santosh to the police station and warned him. Priyadarshini was given a personal security officer for her protection.

Soon thereafter, Priyadarshini was found brutally murdered at a relative's house. Santosh was the main suspect from the start as Priyadarshini's relatives knew of his previous conduct. Following Santosh's denial of any wrongdoing on his part, the matter went to trial.

This case fits into the narrative of a rich and powerful father doing everything in his power to subvert the law and protect his son. Santosh Singh was the son of the Commissioner of Police in Delhi. It was noted that the officials of the Delhi police sat on complaints, conspired to conceal evidence and did everything that they were not supposed to do. This could well have closed the chapter without Santosh facing any consequences. But the media rose to the occasion and waged a war.

The additional sessions judge in the case, G.P. Thareja criticized the role of the Delhi police in the trial: 'There has been particular inaction by Delhi Police', he said, while observing that Santosh's father was probably involved in the subversion of the investigation process. The Delhi High Court agreed with the trial court that the police were reluctant to act on the repeated complaints of harassment and stalking against Singh as his father was a senior IPS (Indian Police Service) officer. The verdict stated that 'junior staff [did] not react to complaints against the relatives of their fraternity', and referred to the trial court's observation that the approach and working of the subordinate staff of the Delhi police clearly reflected that the rule of law 'is not meant for those who enforce the law nor for their near relatives'. All of this went against Santosh at the time of the verdict.

Extensive coverage by various news channels and newspapers created pressure on the CBI, which filed an appeal in the Delhi High Court. Due to the intense media scrutiny, the case was heard on a daily basis, and finally the court pronounced Santosh Singh guilty.

The high court noted thirteen circumstances that went against the accused:

1. The accused had been continuously harassing the deceased right from the end of 1994 to January 1996, a few days before her death. Some of these incidents included:

(a) On 25.2.1995, while the deceased was travelling in her car, the accused followed her on his motorcycle and tried to stop the deceased at the traffic point. The accused gave an undertaking to the police, to 'not to harass in future'. After this undertaking the accused was let off by the police.

(b) On 16.8.1995 the accused followed the car of the deceased on his motorcycle up to her residence at Vasant Kunj. The accused tried to break open the door of her residence. This time again the accused gave an undertaking not to have any concern with the deceased in future.

(c) On 6.11.1995 the accused tried to catch hold of the arm of the deceased.

(d) Priyadarshini Mattoo also filed a complaint dated 27.10.1995 to the Dean, Faculty of Law, Campus Law Centre, stating harassment. The accused was advised to desist from such activities. After humiliation, the accused in retaliation made complaints to the authorities of University of Delhi on 30.10.1995 alleging that Mattoo was simultaneously pursuing two courses from University of Delhi i.e. M.Com. and LL.B. in violation of the rules. In pursuance of the complaint, Prof. B.B. Pandey issued show-cause notices to the deceased seeking her explanation. In response Mattoo submitted that she was a student of M. Com. back in 1991. The deceased was yet to appear in LL.B. IIIrd Year examination. Mattoo claimed that the complaint was malicious. Her result of LL.B. 5th Semester examination was withheld by the University of Delhi pending a final decision on the said complaint.

2. The accused had more than once given an undertaking that the accused would not harass the deceased in future while admitting that the accused had been doing so earlier.

3. The motive of the accused was to either have the deceased or to break her.

4. On the day of occurrence, the accused was seen on the premises of Faculty of Law, University of Delhi in the forenoon, where the deceased had gone to attend her class. The accused was no more a student of Faculty of Law at that time.

5. At the crucial time before murder, i.e., about 5 p.m. on 23.1.1996, the accused was seen outside the door of the flat of Priyadarshini with a helmet in his hand, which had a visor.

6. On the day of occurrence of the murder, the accused had reached late to attend class at Indian Law Institute, Bhagwan Dass Road, where the accused was a student too.

7. Immediately after the murder, the mother of the deceased had raised a suspicion that the accused had a hand in the murder of her daughter.

8. When the accused joined investigation on the night between 23/24.1.1996, the accused had an injury on his right hand. There was swelling and fracture on 5th metacarpal of his right hand. There was no plaster or bandage on his hand. That injury was fresh, having been caused 24 to 38 hours earlier. The blood pressure of the accused at that time was also high, which showed anxiety.

9. DNA and finger-printing tests conclusively established the guilt of the accused.

10. On 25.1.1996, the helmet of the accused, which was taken into possession, had a broken visor. On 23.1.1996 before the murder, it was found by Shri Kuppuswami and Personal Security Officer

Rajinder Singh that the helmet of the accused had a visor. Violence was detected on both sides of visor. Helmet was besmeared with a speck of blood. At the scene of crime, pieces of visor were found near the body of Mattoo smeared with her blood.

11. The deceased had 19 injuries on her besides three broken ribs. These injuries were suggestive of force used for rape. A tear mark over the area of left breast region on the T-shirt of the deceased suggested that the force was used for molestation.

12. The accused took a false defence that fracture on the hand of the accused was sustained on 14.1.1996 and it was not a fresh injury. The accused also gave false replies against proved facts.

13. The influence of the father of the accused resulting in deliberate spoiling of the case.

One of the main failures of the Central Bureau of Investigation (CBI) was its inability to produce Virender Prasad, the domestic help in the house where Priyadarshini was found dead. The Delhi High Court wondered whether this had 'resulted in obstructing the ball of proof of criminal justice from going beyond reasonable doubt due to lack of fairness on part of the CBI in producing such evidence for judicial scrutiny/review'. The CBI recorded Prasad's statement but could not produce him in court as a witness. However, Virender Prasad was easily tracked down at his village by a media house.

According to the trial court, the conduct of the prosecution should have been rooted in the principles of fairness and good sense. However, they conclusively and continuously tried to impede the investigation. The judge held that due to the CBI failing to produce relevant circumstantial evidence in the case, the benefit of the doubt ought to be in favour of Santosh Singh. Thareja, the additional sessions judge, acquitted Singh on the charge of rape and gave him the benefit of the doubt for murder, disregarding the evidence of the expert witness. The trial court rejected the DNA evidence presented before it, contending that it had been tampered with. The high court observed: 'Thus the court is left to consider unfairness on the part of the CBI in keeping the material defence evidence collected by it away from court, created a hole in the proof of the case beyond reasonable doubt.'

In criminal jurisprudence, it seems fair to give the benefit of the doubt to the accused. There are many cases wherein the fault of the investigating agency weakens the case. Unfortunately, in many cases, it seems like a deliberate omission. Should a deliberate default on the part of the investigation agency always go in favour of the accused? That is an unresolved matter of discussion in criminal jurisprudence.

It was reported in various sources that the accused had got married and also become a practising advocate in Delhi itself. On 17 October 2006, Santosh Singh was found guilty under Sections 302 and 376 of the IPC, for murder and rape respectively. The verdict blamed G.P. Thareja's original judgment: 'The trial judge acquitted the accused amazingly taking a perverse approach. It murdered justice and shocked judicial conscience.'

The rape verdict was reversed by the high court: 'Though there appeared to be no physical evidence of rape on the body, but by the DNA test conducted on the vaginal swabs and slides and the underwear of the deceased and the blood sample of the appellant, it was clear that rape had been committed, and that too by him.' The high court held that it would be a dangerous doctrine for the court to discard the evidence of an expert witness by referring to certain texts and books without putting those texts to the expert and taking his opinion. The high court reversed the findings of the trial court that the vaginal swabs and slides and the blood samples of the appellant had been tampered with.

In particular, the verdict held that there was no problem with the DNA testing, and that the combination of the forensic and circumstantial evidence was clinching. The Delhi High Court held that: 'From an overall analysis of the circumstances that have been discussed above and held to have been proved beyond any doubt by unimpeachable evidence, we are of the view that those circumstances form a chain so complete which leads us to the only conclusion that it is the respondent Santosh Singh who had committed rape upon the deceased and then murdered her. The circumstantial evidence in the case is absolutely inconsistent and incompatible with the innocence of the respondent.'

The verdict was reached on the basis of 'conclusive circumstantial evidence'.

In October 2010, the Supreme Court upheld the conviction of Santosh Singh, that even if there was some uncertainty about the rape, there was no question with respect to the culpability of Santosh Singh committing the gruesome murder of Priyadarshini Mattoo. 'Assuming, therefore, for a moment, that there was some uncertainty about the rape, the culpability of the appellant for the murder is nevertheless writ large and we are indeed surprised at the decision of the trial judge in ordering an outright acquittal.'

However, the Supreme Court reduced the death sentence to life imprisonment: 'Undoubtedly, the sentencing part is a difficult one and often exercises the mind of the Court but where the option is between a life sentence and a death sentence, the options are indeed extremely limited, and if the court itself feels some difficulty in awarding one or the other, it is only appropriate that the lesser sentence should be awarded.'

Santosh Singh is currently serving his sentence of life imprisonment.

Jessica Lal

Jessica Lal was a model residing in New Delhi. At a party held near Qutub Minar, she was shot dead by Sidhartha Vashisht, alias Manu Sharma, the son of the then excise minister in Haryana, Venod Sharma. The trial judge acquitted Manu Sharma of the charges levelled against him, but the Delhi High Court found him guilty.

The dispute that arose between Jessica Lal and Manu Sharma, which led to the former being shot at, was trivial. Jessica Lal was serving as a celebrity bartender at the party. Sharma, in an inebriated state, went to Jessica and asked her for a drink. The liquor stock at the party was already over and Jessica told Manu that she would not be able to give him a drink. Manu got angry at this and suddenly brought out a gun. He fired a shot at the ceiling. Immediately after that, he aimed his pistol at Jessica's temple and fired a shot. Jessica died on the spot. Realizing the implications of his act, Manu along with three other associates fled Delhi for Himachal Pradesh the day after the shooting. However, he was caught a few weeks later by the Delhi police.

Most people present at the party refused to provide a testimony of the events of the night. When Sharma shot Jessica, most of the partygoers were present at the venue. However, Manu Sharma and his father had intimidated the potential witnesses into silence by exerting their political influence. As a result, the trial court acquitted Manu Sharma of the charges raised against him on account of insufficient evidence.

Following Sharma's acquittal, there were large-scale public protests demanding justice for Jessica. In Delhi, protests were held near India Gate demanding his conviction. Numerous media houses played their part in the protest, including NDTV, which launched a campaign asking the President of India to intervene in the matter.

Following protests, the case headed for an appeal at the Delhi High Court. In contrast to the lax pace in which proceedings are normally conducted in the high court, this case was tried on a day-to-day basis. The high court found Manu Sharma guilty of murder. On appeal to the Supreme Court, his guilt was upheld and he is currently serving a life-imprisonment term in Tihar Jail.

Manu Sharma was charged with murder and destruction of evidence, among other offences. Sharma's associates were charged with lesser offences, which included conspiracy and harbouring a suspect.

In the initial stages, the trial had been conducted at a snail's pace, which had allowed most witnesses time to withdraw their statements. As many as thirty-two witnesses turned hostile towards the prosecution during the course of the trial; the most prominent among them was actor Shayan Munshi, who was in Jessica's vicinity when she was shot. He had made a statement in Hindi to the police immediately after the shooting. Later, however, he claimed that he did not know Hindi at all and, therefore, the testimony was false. However, his claim was easily countered when a news agency conducted a sting operation in which they asked him to speak in Hindi to check his eligibility for a movie role. Regarding Munshi's testimony that two guns were involved, the judgment stated: 'In court he has taken a somersault and come out with a version that there were two gentlemen at the bar counter . . . We have no manner of doubt that on this aspect he is telling a complete lie.'

In the past, witnesses have been known to retract their statements and give testimony contrary to their own case. Verdicts even make note of this but action is not taken. The law provides for penal action against perjuring witnesses under Section 340 of the CrPC read with Sections 191 to 201 of the IPC, but only in rare cases is any penalty accorded. And this case turned out to be one of those rare cases. Disturbed by the trend of so many of the witnesses turning hostile, the high court, in the appeal against acquittal, initiated suo motu proceedings against the thirty-two witnesses, including Shayan Munshi and ballistics expert P.S. Manocha.

On 20 February 2007, ten of the twenty-nine witnesses were discharged (three of the witnesses had died while the trial was on). On 22 May 2013, the court absolved seventeen more witnesses. However, Munshi and Manocha were directed to be prosecuted for turning hostile.

The Supreme Court in 2016 quashed the perjury case against the ballistics expert, stating, 'It is significant to note that [Manocha's] opinion that the cartridges appeared to have been fired from different firearms was based on the court's insistence to give an opinion without examining the firearm. In other words, it was not even his voluntary, let alone deliberate, deposition.' Perjury charges against Munshi are still pending and he is currently out on bail. A non-bailable warrant issued against him was quashed.

The trial court mentioned that the accused were acquitted because of the Delhi police's failure to produce sufficient evidence, referring to the missing weapon that had been used to fire at Jessica and which was crucial to the prosecution's case. They also failed to prove that the bullets fired at the roof and the one fired at Jessica came from the same weapon.

Media attention grew as the malpractices employed by Manu Sharma to advance his case came to light. On 9 September 2006 a sting operation conducted by the news magazine *Tehelka* aired on STAR News. This appeared to show witnesses being bribed and coerced into retracting their initial testimony. Venod Sharma was named in the exposé as one who had paid money to some of the witnesses. Facing pressure from the high-level Congress leaders, Sharma resigned from the Haryana cabinet.

The Delhi High Court ruled that Sharma was guilty, and criticized the trial judge S.L. Bhayana. Placing ample importance on the testimonies of witnesses Beena Ramani and Deepak Bhojwani, the high court opined that there was non-application of mind on Bhayana's part and he gave the judgment with an intention to acquit Manu Sharma and his associates: 'Obviously, this reflects total lack of application of mind and suggests a hasty approach towards securing a particular end, namely, the acquittals.'

During the proceedings, a typical third-party defence was also raised. Senior advocate Ram Jethmalani argued in favour of the accused and put forward the theory that it was a 'tall Sikh man' other than Amardeep Singh Gill (the co-accused), who had fired the bullets that killed Jessica, and not his client Manu Sharma. Jethmalani supported his two-weapon theory with the aid of ballistics experts and Shayan Munshi, who had turned hostile and had stated that the bullet that hit Jessica had not been fired by Manu Sharma but someone else. While Deepak Bhojwani had said that while he was moving around in the party, he came in contact with Sharma, who requested him to arrange liquor for him, following which he told him that the bar had closed. Then one 'Sikh gentleman' came from behind Sharma and told him something and took him away towards Tamarind Court, and correctly identified the pictures of Manu Sharma and the tall Sikh man as Amardeep Singh Gill (the co-accused), Ram Jethmalani urged the court to discard the statements of Bhojwani on the grounds that he was an interested party who had been friends with Jessica for five to six years. He also argued that Bhojwani was not on the list of invitees and had been planted to favour the prosecution version.

The Supreme Court held, in absence of rebuttal evidence: 'The entire premise of the defence argument that it was not a person in a white T-shirt, stocky and fair, who shot at Jessica Lal over a row over the drink and fled away from the spot, and this was a planted and concocted story of the prosecution to rope in Manu Sharma and make escape good of the tall Sikh gentleman is wholly erroneous and without any basis.'

One of the main aspects of the case was the testimony of Beena Ramani, the owner of Tamarind Court, the restaurant where the fateful incident had taken place. The trial court discarded the statements made by Ramani where she has claimed that she saw the victim falling down as she ran into the accused, as she was not an eyewitness to the occurrence, but accepted that she was a witness to the presence of Manu Sharma. The Supreme Court agreed with the findings of the Delhi High Court. The latter conveyed its displeasure, and said, 'The trial court went totally wrong in holding that Beena Ramani had admitted not seeing Manu Sharma firing a shot at Jessica Lal, but it was only her feeling. With great respect to the learned Judge, we find this is "a complete misreading of evidence".' It also went on to say, 'This kind of approach of the trial court has caused a grave miscarriage of justice.' The Supreme Court of India rejected the allegations of the

Ramani family being under pressure to stick to the police version of events.

Ultimately, Manu Sharma was fined and awarded life imprisonment. The other accused were fined and given four years' rigorous imprisonment. A plea for Sharma to be sentenced to death was rejected on the grounds that the murder, although intentional, was not premeditated, and Sharma was not considered to be a threat to society.

Sharma's lawyer announced that the decision would be appealed in the Supreme Court because the judgment was wrong in treating Beena Ramani as a witness.

Jethmalani assailed the Delhi High Court verdict, alleging that the media had prejudged the issue and conducted a campaign to vilify his client. The Supreme Court accepted that there had been an element of 'trial by media' but believed that it had not affected the decision of the high court.

On 19 April 2010, the Supreme Court upheld the verdict—the evidence regarding the actual incident, the testimonies of the witnesses, the evidence connecting the vehicles and cartridges to the accused, Manu Sharma, and his conduct after the incident proved his guilt beyond reasonable doubt.

A Reasonably Free Convict

Sidhartha Vashisht, alias Manu Sharma, has drawn attention to himself for all the wrong reasons. Since his conviction in 2006, Manu Sharma has often enjoyed the joys of the outside world. He has been involved in a brawl with the son of the police commissioner of Delhi, attended family functions and even visited a nightclub. He defied authorities and was guilty of disruptive behaviour, even after his conviction, probably a result of the heady combination of money and power he enjoyed as the son of a well-connected and high-ranking politician and the owner of four hotels and three sugar mills. Manu was granted parole more frequently than he should have been because of his family connections. On 24 September 2009, he was granted parole for a period of thirty days for the cited reasons of looking after the family business, caring for his ailing mother and attending the last rites of his grandmother. To no one's surprise, Manu Sharma again became the centre of controversy after it emerged that his grandmother, whose last rites he had so dearly wished to attend, had passed away in 2008. The claim of his mother being ill was also proved false after she was seen perfectly fit trying to promote a ladies' cricket event in Chandigarh. Even after such revelations, Sharma was seen partying in a Delhi discotheque, after his parole has been extended for thirty more days. After an uproar that he had violated parole norms, Sharma had to surrender to the jail authorities two weeks before the expiry of his parole period. Manu Sharma showed no sign of remorse or regret, and consequently the court made a conscious effort to restrict his movements during his subsequent parole applications, making arrangements to ensure he adhered to the conditions.

During his time in prison, Manu Sharma obtained a number of educational degrees, including a postgraduate degree in human rights law and a bachelor's in law. Needless to say, he was granted parole to appear for his examinations. Most recently, in April 2015, Manu Sharma was released on furlough (a leave of absence) and not parole, which requires legal sanction, to attend his own wedding in Chandigarh

The criminal justice system suffers from chronic favouritism—so much so that the law is seen by many of the country's poor as a tool merely for the rich and powerful. High-profile lawbreakers get away scot-free. Recently, Salman Khan procured bail in his case only hours after being convicted in Mumbai, even though thousands of ordinary inmates wait for years to get bail. In the backdrop of this perception, the Priyadarshini Mattoo and Jessica Lal cases are the torchbearers for justice for all.

The role of the media in bringing to the fore public opinion is crucial. Without the role of media groups such as Tehelka and NDTV, neither Santosh Singh nor Manu Sharma would have been brought to justice as promptly as they were. In both the cases, matters escalated and courts took serious note only after the extensive media speculation and resultant public furore. One can well imagine how long the trials might have stretched on for otherwise. Therefore, a robust judicial system is needed to reverse acquittals.

Failures on the investigation level and general incompetence on the part of the officials involved in the case are another pitfall of the criminal justice system. In both Priyadarshini Mattoo's and Jessica Lal's cases, key police officials blundered at crucial stages of the investigation. Whether it was with regard to the recording of witness statements or the collection of evidence, the police failed to deliver. This was amply demonstrated in Priyadarshini Mattoo's case, when the police all but refused to search for the domestic help who had seen Priyadarshini's killer near the site of the murder on the day of her death. Suffice it to say that low criminal convictions invariably happen due to defective and inefficient investigations. The game is over before the trial even begins.

6

IN THE NAME OF GOD: TERRORISM

In our world, communication has come to play an important role in the commission of terrorist crimes. Terrorists have become aware of the risks of leaving a *digital footprint*, which could leave a trail for the enforcement agencies, and thus look to old forms of communication such as using messenger birds that don't leave any lasting digital trace. One of the reasons it took so long for US intelligence to track down Osama bin Laden, was because he relied on the age-old method of delivering messages and data by hand. Terrorists today use a mix of both old and modern forms of communication, making messages even more difficult to intercept.

Almost all current forms of digital communication are encrypted. The fact that general modes of communication are extremely secure now also aids secure communication for terrorists. It is estimated that about 70 per cent of the content released by the Islamic State is first published on Twitter. Similarly, in the 26/11 terrorist attack case, it was reported that Indian SIM cards purchased near the Bangladesh border were used by terrorists. Often, the cards would be used for a few days and then disposed of to avoid being traced. The handlers in Pakistan used satellite phones to talk to the terrorists and guide them during the three-day ordeal. Information as well as moral support to further their objective was obtained from media broadcasts. To confuse authorities, the attackers contacted media channels and asked for ransom to make them believe that they were dealing with a hostage situation and not a terrorist attack. Modern-day communication methods and mass media have thus come to play a central role in the successful execution of terrorist offences. These new-age interactive communication systems have enabled terrorism to take on the role of a many-headed hydra—as soon as we develop the technology to cut off one head, another takes its place—and it has become a bigger threat today than the world has ever seen.

Unique Features of Antiterrorism Laws

Terrorism has attracted a unique jurisprudence all over the world. The dominant principle that is applied is that the laws should reflect the mood of the nation and that of the global state to eliminate sheer evil. This category of laws proceeds on certain assumptions. One such assumption is that by nature, terrorism is an act born out of conspiracy. The plan to commit the act is formulated by someone in location X and is executed by someone else thousands of miles away in location Y. This makes it difficult to find direct evidence against the conspirators. For instance, in the context of the Mumbai blasts of 1993, David Headley and Tiger Memon were key to the plot but incarcerating them became problematic.

When Lashkar-e-Taiba's (LeT) plan started to materialize in 2007, Headley was considered ideal to complete the reconnaissance missions as he was a foreigner and wouldn't attract too much unwanted attention. With the Rs 15 lakh that was given to him, Headley opened a front office in Mumbai, ostensibly, of an immigration business. Headley had previously used such offices to traffic heroin. In 2007 and 2008, Headley came to Mumbai five times to hunt for locations where the terrorists would carry out the multipronged attack. Despite such direct involvement in the conspiracy, his conviction by American courts was a burdensome affair.

Likewise, in the context of the 1993 Mumbai blasts, Tiger Memon was one of the prime accused. He smuggled weapons into the country via the sea route and also planned the attack. However, he was never physically caught by the enforcement authorities. The kingpin in most cases is only identified after tracing a long trail of events and evidence. This made his capture next to impossible.

Laws have to be formulated in a manner which will enable them to, despite a lack of direct evidence, tackle issues that disturb the very foundation of a country. It is necessary for them to take a perspective that perceives the social implications of the offence and values the disposition of the world to eliminate the wrongs against humanity, irrespective of all odds.

The courts too have to deal with the issue holistically. For instance, many a time, the potential reporting of terrorist acts instils fear in the minds of the general population. Live reporting can even be counterproductive; the 26/11 Mumbai blasts are a case in point, wherein broadcasting of the events made it difficult for task forces to capture the terrorists. It enabled their handlers sitting across the border to guide them, step by step, pursuant to the knowledge gained after watching the news footage. Abu Jundal, the Hindi tutor of the terrorists, told his interrogators that the careless live reporting of the events by certain sections of the Indian media was an advantage to the terrorists and helped foil the attempts of the National Security Guard at rescue. The Supreme Court, in such a situation, rightly pulled up the media for its lackadaisical attitude and affirmed that any effort to defend the behaviour of the TV channels by citing the right to freedom of speech and expression would be incorrect and unacceptable.

A colonial hangover of criminal jurisprudence is that confessions made before a police officer are inadmissible under the Indian Evidence Act, 1872. As evidence against terrorists is hardly ever gathered easily, confessions are integral to these cases. Therefore, antiterror laws, generally, depending on the backdrop of the type of crime, hold such confessions admissible under the Terrorism and Disruptive Activities (Prevention) Act, 1987 (TADA), and the Prevention of Terrorism Act, 2002 (POTA). To refute the veracity of the statement, the accused has to prove that the confession has been obtained from him or her by inducement or threat by a person in authority. The burden of proof is thus shifted.

Another striking feature of the law in our country is that the nature of bail is intrinsically different in the case of terrorist crimes. An accused terrorist has no inherent right of bail. The Unlawful Activities Prevention Act, 1968, allows detention without filing of a charge sheet for up to 180 days without any provision of bail. Even otherwise, accused terrorists are most unlikely to get bail thereafter, on account of the nature of their crime.

Global Decimation

The attacks on the World Trade Centre in New York on 11 September 2001—or '9/11'—were the first major terrorist attacks that caught the attention of the entire world due to their sheer massive scale and magnitude.

In the immediate aftermath of the attacks, al-Qaeda leadership posted videos via Al Jazeera, a Qatar-based broadcasting channel. The channel edited and selected only a few of the videos before broadcasting them. An unhappy al-Qaeda then switched to uploading videos themselves on the Internet. Since then, these organizations have developed their own production houses, producing and disseminating content with high production value.

Pursuant to 9/11, the world has been divided into, according to the United States, good and evil. This distinction brings forth interventions—even pre-emptive in nature—in the Middle East, the hotbed of terrorism.

The power game is much bigger than just the al-Qaeda. ISIS, now a global threat, aims to create a Sunni Muslim state. Having claimed responsibility for the suicide bombing in Paris in 2015, the Charlie Hebdo shooting in 2015 and the recent Manchester concert attack of May 2017, among many others, its radical views now very seriously threaten the current state structure and boundaries.

In India, too, the situation is not very different. The invasive attack by members of the Jaish-e-Mohammed at the Pathankot air force base in 2016 took advantage of the porous borders of Punjab, and was carried out with the objective of disrupting peace talks between India and Pakistan while simultaneously destroying a military airbase. India claims that an attack of this magnitude could not have taken place without the knowledge of Pakistan's intelligence agency, the Inter-Services Intelligence, or ISI, and the Pakistan government.

In such a situation, it is encouraging that the heads of both countries are working hand in hand to defeat the terrorists' motives. It was reported in news outlets that Prime Minister Narendra Modi cautiously commented, 'Today, enemies of humanity who can't see India progress tried to strike at our strategic area, a prominent airbase at Pathankot.' The Pakistani government condemned the attack in an unprecedented move and arrested the leader of Jaish-e-Mohammed in an effort to show its seriousness about cooperating with India. Such collaboration and harmony is the cornerstone of a terrorism-free world.

With time, terrorism has become a commonplace and global phenomenon. People from all strata of society—

the poor, rich, educated and illiterate—are affected or participating in it. Educated people becoming victims of propaganda shows the alarming proportions the problem has assumed. Engineers and college students adopting radical paths after being subjected to the lure of ISIS propaganda techniques are proof that some people's perception of the terror outfit's fundamentalist acts is changing. In such a scenario, there is no denying that the situation is grave and demands immediate global attention and collective cooperation.

Pointed Guns at Parliament

A gory case in point is the Afzal Guru—or Parliament attack—case. The national capital witnessed an unprecedented attack on the afternoon of 13 December 2001. Five heavily armed men with massive firepower at their disposal barged into Parliament while it was in session, in a car fitted with a bomb, covered in home-ministry and Parliament security labels. Inflicting numerous casualties en route, the group crashed their vehicle into the then vice president Krishan Kant's official vehicle and began firing indiscriminately. As recorded by the Delhi High Court, 'The firepower was awesome. Enough to engage a battalion. Had the terrorists succeeded, the entire building with all inside would have perished. The foundation of the country would have shaken. The act was clearly an act of waging war against the Government of India.'

The Indian security personnel retaliated, leading to a fierce thirty-minute-long gun battle. Eight security personnel and a gardener were martyred in the attacks. However, all the members of Parliament escaped unhurt. Had the men succeeded in the attack, the iconic Parliament House would have been reduced to ashes and scores of lives would have been lost.

Two days after the incident, the special cell of the Delhi police found clues from the call detail records of the mobile phones and from the registration of the vehicle used in the attack. These led to the arrest of Afzal Guru, an unassuming commission agent in the fruit business and later an area manager for a pharmaceutical firm. Three others, namely, Shaukat Hussain Guru (Afzal's cousin), Shaukat's wife, Afsan Guru, aka Navjot Sandhu, and S.A.R. Geelani, a lecturer of Arabic at Delhi University, were also arrested. A seventeen-day-long extensive investigation proved the involvement of members of the banned militant organization Jaish-e-Mohammed.

This case is also relevant from the perspective of media interference in judicial trials. Afzal raised concerns over not getting a fair trial as the media had created a public furore and already declared him a criminal, but his complaint fell on deaf ears. Amidst such allegations of a 'trial by media', the special court, presided over by Justice S.N. Dhingra, concluded the trial at lightning speed. In a short span of six months, over 300 documents, eighty witnesses for the prosecution and ten witnesses on behalf of the accused, S.A.R. Geelani, were examined and the sentence pronounced. Afzal Guru, S.A.R. Geelani and Shaukat Hussain Guru were sentenced to death on 18 December 2002.

The trial was marred by reports of evidence tampering. The two most important pieces of evidence against Guru—a cell phone and a laptop confiscated at the time of arrest—were not sealed. Evidence, when collected, is required to be sealed at the site from where it is obtained, sent for analysis and ultimately stored. In this case, the laptop was accessed after the arrest. However, it was clarified later that it was operated by independent agencies and there was nothing to show that the evidence had been tampered with.

The laptop contained incriminating evidence, such as fake home-ministry passes. The Supreme Court relied on this evidence and remarked, 'It is established from the evidence that the said laptop was used for the preparation of the I-cards, and the I-cards found at the spot on the dead bodies and the MHA [Ministry of Home Affairs] sticker found on the car were those produced from the same laptop. It admits of no doubt that the laptop, which must have been with the deceased terrorist Mohammad and others, came into the custody of Afzal (and Shaukat) soon after the incident on December 13 and such possession has not been accounted for.'

Afzal's confession statement to the police was also questioned. The police handcuffed Afzal and called the media to broadcast his 'confession' to the world. Such a confession is, however, inadmissible as evidence in the court of law. The assistant commissioner of police, Rajbir Singh, in charge of the case, in his testimony, stated, 'I allowed the media to interview the accused Afzal in my office under the consent of my senior officer, namely the deputy commissioner of police [DCP].'

Though access to information is essential for a healthy democracy, when such access invades the judicial process, it attacks the core of the democratic process. The increased invasion of the fourth estate may at times hinder the functioning of the judiciary. However, the high court dismissed the contention that the broadcast of the statement caused prejudice in the minds of judges and the general public. The court noted, 'There is nothing on record that the atmosphere was not free from threat or inducement.' Relying on the Supreme Court judgment of *R. Balakrishna Pillai v. State of Kerala*,[1] which held that judges do not get influenced by propaganda or adverse publicity, the high court opined that judges are trained, skilled and have sufficient experience to shut their minds to hearsay or influence from media reports.

It is interesting to note that the trial court admitted the confession statement. However, the Supreme Court didn't give any weight to the same as procedural safeguards were not complied with and proceeded on the basis of other evidence. The government passed the Prevention of Terrorism Ordinance (POTO) (later enacted by Parliament as POTA) on 19 December, i.e., after the 13 December attack, and it was applied to this case on a retrospective basis. The POTO/POTA makes confessions made before police officers admissible, but with some safeguards. One of those is the right to counsel, which was denied to Afzal. The second is the right to adequate time for reflection before signing the statement. This was also, in the Supreme Court's opinion, not provided. Afzal took seven months to refute and then retract his statement. However, the

Supreme Court opined, 'We cannot hold that there was abnormal delay in disowning the confession, the effect of which would be to impart credibility to the confessional statement.'

Tactics and Finances: Running the Terrorism Business

The aim of terrorism today has become to grab and hold the world's attention while making use of psychological tactics to instil fear and threaten international order. We, in our anxiousness and fear, tend to contribute to this by exaggerating their power and strength in our minds. The acts of terrorists are consciously orchestrated so that media houses—print, television and social—publicize the event.

While a terrorist organization must have followers and a motivational ideology, it must also have a basic structure to feed itself and its recruiters. Adequate finances ensure that its recruiters and their families are cared for and have enough equipment, arms and ammunition to further their cause. Terrorist organizations spend substantial amounts to sustain their influence and govern their troops. According to a report by the Asian Development Bank, maintenance and administration expenses constitute about 90 per cent of al-Qaeda's total income, whereas only 10 per cent is spent on operational purposes.

Moving physical cash is a logistical nightmare for these organizations. $1 million (about Rs 7 crore) in $100 bills weighs about 10 kg. To overcome this problem, ingenious ways of transportation are often adopted. After the 9/11 attacks, US federal agents received a tip-off that a Yemeni sheikh was raising money in Brooklyn for al-Qaeda. He had supposedly bragged in recorded chats of having raised $20 million for Osama bin Laden. Allegedly, some of this money was raised in cash donations. The sheikh shipped the bulk cash in cargo vessels. Federal agents later arrested two men at John F. Kennedy Airport in New York in October 2001 and found $140,000 hidden in cardboard boxes alongside jars of honey.

In the Mumbai terror attacks, the Intelligence Bureau concluded that the LeT had spent Rs 1,17,37,820 on the attacks. Such huge amounts of money come from money laundering, arms proliferation, smuggling of narcotics, and so on. On the other hand, kidnappings, ransom, looting and marauding along with extortion are just some of the ways that ISIS has adopted to supplement their income from oil wells. They have even begun to tax people for money. Many families even choose to trade their children for money. Born into a humble family, with a snack-cart-owner father and labourer brother, Ajmal Kasab couldn't get much of an education and was a class-four dropout. He spoke a smattering of rough Hindi and no English. Though his father denies it, it is alleged that Kasab's father sold him to the LeT to support his family. Various sources put the amount paid by the terror group for his participation in the attacks at between Rs 1–2.5 lakh. There are also reports of him living in Okara village of the Punjab province in Pakistan six months prior to the attack. It is alleged by villagers that he took his mother's blessings before he left for his mission to India.

Mental and physical training also plays a key role in the commission of terrorist offences. In the context of the 26/11 incident, Kasab and the other members of his group received training from the LeT in using arms and ammunition, marine warfare and marine navigation in Muzaffarabad in Kashmir.

The young recruits were given psychological training to strengthen their minds and imbibe radical ideologies, and physical combat training to strengthen their bodies. Out of this group of twenty-four men, ten were chosen for the Mumbai mission. The extent of their mental training is seen from the fact that these terrorists are unaffected by their actions. The Supreme Court bench too expressed concern at Kasab's remorselessness. Kasab's young age, as highlighted by the amicus curiae to the case, senior advocate Raju Ramachandran, did not affect the decision of the bench, given the nature of the crime. In this regard the bench observed that the 'only mitigating factor is the appellant's young age, but that is completely offset by the absence of any remorse on his part, and the resultant finding that in his case there is no possibility of any reformation or rehabilitation'.

Outraged by the attacks, many lawyers initially refused to represent Kasab, thereby delaying his trial. The Bombay Bar Association passed a resolution that none of its members would represent him. Though there was enough prima facie evidence, we, a democratic nation, upheld the values of equity and justice we hold so dear and gave Kasab a proper judicial trial.

He was charged with murder, waging war against India and other ancillary charges in an 11,000-page charge sheet filed by the Mumbai police. His trial began in May 2009. In an attempt to throw the authorities off their game, Kasab claimed to be only seventeen years old on the first day of the trial and requested to be tried in a juvenile court. Had this request been entertained, Kasab could have succeeded in being awarded a much more lenient punishment.

Initially he pleaded not guilty before the trial court, but in a turn of events in July 2009, he admitted to his guilt. He emphasized, 'If I am hanged for this, I am not bothered. I don't want any mercy from the court.' Affording him a fair trial, the judge opined that the trial should continue despite his admission of guilt. Alleging that he had been tortured by the Mumbai police, Kasab later retracted his confession statements. He claimed that he had been unjustly arrested and was framed and picked up by the Mumbai police from a beach. He also claimed that he had come to the city to pursue his education and had never seen an AK-47 rifle.

In March 2010, the trial concluded and Kasab was found guilty of all eighty-six charges and sentenced to death, which was confirmed by the Bombay High Court. The high court recorded: '[The confession statement] will show that these terrorists were proceeding via Chowpatty towards Malabar Hill, which was their final target . . . Kasab waged a war against the Government of India, pursuant to a conspiracy which was hatched in Pakistan . . . There is hardly any scope for a person like Kasab to be rehabilitated or reformed.'

In the appeal, the Supreme Court held:

In short, this is a case of terrorist attack from across the border. It has a magnitude of unprecedented enormity on all scales. The conspiracy behind the attack was as deep and large as it was vicious. The preparation and training for the execution was as thorough as the execution was ruthless . . . This case has the element of conspiracy as no other case. The appellant was part of a conspiracy hatched across the border to wage war against the Government of India, and lethal arms and explosives were collected with the intention of waging war against the Government of India.

Upholding the death sentence, the Supreme Court recorded that:

[The] enormity of the crime in all scales . . . in terms of loss of life and property, and more importantly in its traumatizing effect, this case stands alone, or it is at least the very rarest of rare to come before this court since the birth of the republic. Therefore, it should attract the rarest of rare punishment . . . As long as the death penalty remains on the statute book as punishment for certain offences, including waging war and murder, it logically follows that there must be some cases, howsoever rare or one in a million, that would call for inflicting that penalty . . . That being the position, we fail to see what case would attract the death penalty, if not the case of the appellant. To hold back the death penalty in this case would amount to obdurately declaring that this court rejects death as lawful penalty even though it is on the statute book and held valid by constitutional benches of this court.

As all accused do in death-sentence cases, Kasab too sought to exhaust all the legal remedies at his disposal and filed a mercy petition. The President of India dismissed the petition, casting Kasab's ultimate fate in stone. The trial took over four years and cost the Government of India about Rs 60 crore. Despite the huge financial and emotional cost associated with this trial, a terrorist was given protection and a fair chance to defend himself before the Indian courts of law, upholding the virtues of democracy and rule of law prevalent in our nation.

Kasab was secretly hanged in the premises of Yerwada Central Jail, Pune, and his body buried in an unmarked location. Even the media was kept in the dark about his execution and was only informed about one hour after he was buried. It is stated that he hardly slept the night before his execution and sang throughout. He was apparently surprisingly calm when brought for execution and displayed no sign of nervousness. Dressed in jail clothes, just before his hanging, he sought forgiveness from the divine—for an act that only the divine could possibly forgive.

While the world is working towards breaking down terrorism, it becomes impossible to rip it apart from its roots due to various reasons. The ideology is deep-rooted and is gaining popular support among those who can be misled, those who have lost faith in the current government and bureaucratic system, those who have been let down by them, or those who have suffered any kind of mishap, such as losing their jobs, families or ideologies due to certain government policies. These factors make terrorism a complex issue that is persistent and difficult to tackle.

The idea of terrorism may be twofold. It may be revolutionary or an inherently destructive and selfish one, determined from the objectives, motives and aims of the people carrying out any such acts.

The objectives sought to be achieved range from ethnocentric to secessionist and nationalistic to revolutionary. These terrorists may be viewed by some as saviours, who, in the face of all odds, are bringing to people a ray of light. This brings us to their changing roles and perception in the eyes of people. Terrorist psychology is not an irrational one. Motivations could be religious, political, social or economic, or to show solidarity with other terrorists in the name of an ideological agenda. While this may be a goal in transnational terrorist organizations, in South Asian countries, most people merely treat it as a job they must do in order to earn money, with little or no political motives.

In any case, terrorism is a social menace that threatens the very foundation of a civilized society. It is against humanist ethics, and to treat the resultant civilian casualties as justifiable or inevitable is to regard innocent lives as expendable. For civilization to thrive, it is essential that terrorism is removed from the world.

7

NANAVATI: THE END OF JURY TRIALS IN INDIA

Indian viewers of Western legal television dramas such as *Boston Legal* and *The Practice* may have often wondered about jury trials wherein ordinary citizens sit in a box, listen carefully to every word being uttered by the prosecution and defence, and eventually deliver a collective verdict. The inevitable follow-up question is: Why does the American system have trial by jury and not the Indian system? The answer can be found in the case of K.M. Nanavati and its aftermath. Why was Nanavati let off by the jury? Was it swayed by public sentiment, morality, sympathy or some other factor?

Before we go into the almost Bollywood-esque facts of the case, let's take a brief look at the origin and subsequent evolution of jury trials over the centuries.

The History of Jury Trials

As is true for quite a few inventions, it is difficult to answer with certainty who the first people were to hold trial by jury. The current toss-up is between the Anglo-Saxons and the Normans. But the modern-day jury system indisputably owes its origin largely to the legal innovations of King Henry II, who was the monarch of England from 1154–89.

In the seventeenth and eighteenth centuries, the expansion of the British Empire to a scale where the sun never set upon it led to the spread of English culture to different parts of the world. Slowly, the colonies also adopted the British way of administering justice and dispute resolution, including trial by jury. The inhabitants of the new republic in America took a particular liking to the jury system. Thomas Jefferson described trial by jury as 'the only anchor ever yet imagined by man by which a government can be held to the principles of its constitution'.

In the case of India, by the middle of the nineteenth century, the British rule over the subcontinent was almost absolute and, as a result, trial by jury became a regular feature of the Indian legal system, incorporated in Chapter 23 of the Code of Criminal Procedure, 1861; this code was repealed and a fresh code effected, titled the Code of Criminal Procedure (CrPC) in 1973.

K.M. Nanavati v. State of Maharashtra

The case had all the hallmarks of a Bollywood drama (and it was turned into one)—a decorated Parsi naval officer, a beautiful wife, a notorious playboy businessman and an affair. This was perhaps the first time in independent India when the media was so engrossed in a legal case that all the principal actors—the accused, the witnesses as well as the lawyers—had become household names. Millennials who have grown up with constant coverage of the Aarushi murder case would be surprised to find that even sixty years ago, society's appetite for a salacious murder case was not too different. The major difference would be that now television media has replaced the role print media used to play. A sensational 'crime of passion' involving the crème de la crème of Bombay—the case of Nanavati, where a highly decorated naval officer shot his wife's paramour in 1959—is indelibly inked in the annals of the city's history. A case that garnered unprecedented media attention and support for the accused, it is most significant in legal chronicles as being the last in India to be heard as a jury trial.

Kawas Manekshaw Nanavati was a naval commander working with the Indian Navy. Second in command at the *INS Mysore*, he married an Englishwoman named Sylvia in 1949 and together they had three children. After his service led the family to different places around the country, the family finally settled in Bombay in the early 1950s. Around this time, Sylvia and Kawas Nanavati met Prem Bhagwandas Ahuja, a Karachi émigré who owned an automobile business in the city. Prem Ahuja was a regular face in the upper echelons of Bombay society and also notorious for the affairs he had with the wives of the officers of the armed forces.

Nanavati was required to leave his family for long durations due to the nature of his service. Somewhere around 1957, Sylvia Nanavati and Prem Ahuja formed a friendship, which eventually developed into an intimate relationship. On returning home in April 1959, Nanavati, then thirty-seven, found his wife very distant and forlorn. When he inquired into the matter, Sylvia confessed to the affair. An agitated Nanavati was furious. Feeling hopeless, he expressed the desire to put an end to his life. Sylvia then entreated him to let 'bygones be bygones' and not contemplate killing himself. After lunch that day, Nanavati drove his wife and children to the Metro Cinema for a matinee show, his demeanour betraying no signs of his intentions. After dropping them off at the cinema, he drove to his ship, which was docked at Bombay Harbour, informed the captain that he intended to drive to Ahmednagar and requested permission to withdraw a revolver with six rounds for safety purposes. Putting the gun in an envelope, Nanavati drove to Universal Motors on Peddar Road, a showroom Ahuja owned. When Nanavati did not find him there, he proceeded to Jeevan Jyoti Apartments in Setalvad Lane near Malabar Hill, where Prem Ahuja lived with his sister, Mamie.

Nanavati was let into the third-floor flat by the housemaid. He walked into Ahuja's bedroom, where he found him just coming out of his bath. What happened next was the main matter of dispute at the trial. The defence claimed that Nanavati placed the envelope containing the revolver on a table. He wanted to know if Ahuja would marry his wife and take responsibility for the children.

To this, Ahuja is said to have replied, 'Will I marry every woman I sleep with?' Ahuja then spotted the weapon and moved towards it. Nanavati followed and, in the ensuing scuffle, three shots went off, killing Prem Ahuja.

The prosecution claimed that Nanavati had gone to Ahuja's flat with the premeditated intention of killing him. It was asserted that upon reaching the apartment, Nanavati shot Ahuja three times in cold blood.

Nanavati then left the flat without explaining anything to a frantic Mamie Ahuja, who found her brother sprawled on the floor of his bedroom, clad in a towel. The officer then unloaded the gun, headed straight to Commander Samuel, the provost marshal of the Western Naval Command, to confess, and, on the latter's advice, turned himself in at the nearby Gamdevi police station.

Pursuant to his surrender, Nanavati was put on trial under Sections 302 and 304 of the IPC. Under the first section, he would be tried for murder, punishable by death or life imprisonment. Under the second section, he would be charged with culpable homicide, meaning an act executed in the 'heat of the moment', possibly leading to the awarding of a maximum punishment of ten years, or even the possibility of acquittal. The dilemma before the court was whether the murder was indeed an impulsive act carried out under provocation or a premeditated one.

The case was presented in the Bombay sessions court in May 1959. Nanavati pleaded not guilty, and his defence team, comprising Karl Khandalavala, Rajni Patel and S.R. Vakil, argued culpable homicide. Chandu Trivedi, advised by Ram Jethmalani, formed the prosecution, arguing that this was a premeditated murder. In the sessions court, headed by Ratilal Mehta, a cosmopolitan jury consisting of nine members was instated.

Meanwhile, outside the courtroom, the case was picked up by Russi Karanjia, editor of a weekly tabloid called *Blitz*. Karanjia portrayed his fellow Parsi Nanavati as an upright and honourable middle-class gentleman who had acted against a degenerate member of the bourgeois. Karanjia lost no time in according maximum coverage to this case in his tabloid. Accompanying it were images that presented Nanavati in the best light possible. The story was lapped up by all classes of Bombay society, boosting sales for *Blitz* and spawning other opportunistic ventures—such as Ahuja towels and Nanavati toy guns—by other enterprising persons.

In the collective consciousness, the case began to take shape as an honour killing; the personal animosity between Nanavati and Ahuja mushroomed to engulf both the Parsi and Sindhi communities, to which the accused and victim belonged, respectively. The Parsi community came out in passionate support of Nanavati as a hero championing the cause of honour and marital fidelity, as did the public at large, owing mainly to the sensational coverage by *Blitz*. Sylvia, in spite of their recent history, stood beside her husband like a rock. She regularly attended court proceedings and testified in favour of Nanavati. Consumed by guilt for having broken her marital vows and wronging an honourable man, Sylvia, clad in a white sari, cut a demure figure in court.

As was the practice, the trial was opened by the public prosecutor, C.M. Trivedi. To everyone's surprise, in a volte-face, he argued that it was a case of culpable homicide and not of murder. Ram Jethmalani, who, on Mamie Ahuja's prodding, had been helping the prosecution put together a winnable case, was shocked at this sudden turn of events. Incensed, he decided to leave the legal team. But Trivedi, realizing his mistake, managed to convince Jethmalani to stay on. After a long-winded trial, in which the arguments of both the sides were concluded, the jury began its deliberations and, along with the jury, so did the entire city of Bombay. By virtue of the inexhaustible media coverage, the trial virtually played out in front of the entire city and, hence, everyone had an opinion on the fate that should befall Nanavati.

While the judge's role was confined to deciding the issue on law, the jury was supposed to interpret the facts and pronounce a verdict of guilty or not guilty on the charges of murder pressed against Nanavati. However, the media uproar surrounding the issue had polarized public opinion across the state. The public interest was such that people took leave from work to watch every proceeding, gathering in large numbers outside the sessions courts. The public pressure and interest was so pronounced and prevalent in this matter that the jury members could hardly decide between fact and fiction.

The jury, comprising all Parsi members, pronounced the accused not guilty in an eight-to-one verdict. This was in spite of incriminating evidence presented by the prosecution, such as the three-hour gap between Sylvia's confession and the time of the murder, the precise bullet shots, and the fact that despite the reported scuffle, the victim's body was found clad in the same manner in which he came out of his shower. This marked a principal conflict between the opinion of the judge and that of the jury. Under suspicion that the jury had been swayed by media-generated sympathy for the accused, Judge Ratilal Mehta deemed the verdict 'perverse'. In his view no reasonable body of people could have arrived on that verdict based on the evidence provided, and so he referred the matter to the Bombay High Court.

However, to prove that the verdict was perverse was easier said than done. High courts were generally very circumspect in admitting such references. In the Bombay High Court, the state was led by Y.V. Chandrachud, who later went on to become the longest-serving Chief Justice of India. To avoid going down the difficult road of proving the verdict 'perverse', the bar for which was set very high, Chandrachud, in a smart move, set about proving that the jury was misdirected by the court. He ventured to show that the Bombay High Court, where the case was presented in the winter of 1959, saw a reiteration of the question between premeditated murder and culpable homicide.

The Bombay High Court dismissed the jury's verdict and held Nanavati to be guilty.

Nanavati appealed to the Supreme Court, contending that under Section 307 of the Code of Criminal Procedure, 1861, the high court was not empowered to set aside the verdict of the jury on the grounds that there was misdirection. The Supreme Court did not agree with this contention. Upon considering the historical background of Section 307, the court observed that the provision confers wide powers of interference on the high court in an appeal to safeguard against an erroneous verdict of the jury.

The court discussed that one of the main considerations in the case was the principle of sudden and grave provocation. If a crime is committed in a fit of rage or passion directly as a result of being provoked to such an extent so as to make a normal person lose all sense of logic and belief, fly into a rage and commit the said act without thinking, then it shall be an exception and count as a provocation.

As held by the Supreme Court, the test of 'grave and sudden provocation' is whether a reasonable man, belonging to the same class of society to which the accused belongs, and placed in the situation in which the accused was placed, would be so provoked as to lose his self-control.

- In India, words or gestures may also, under certain circumstances, cause grave and sudden provocation to an accused so as to bring it within the first exception to Section 300 of the IPC.
- The mental background created by the previous act of the victim may be taken into consideration in ascertaining whether the subsequent act caused grave and sudden provocation for committing the offence.
- The fatal blow should be clearly traced to the influence of passion arising from that provocation and not after the passion had cooled down by

lapse of time, or otherwise by giving room and scope for premeditation and calculation. The accused is presumed to be innocent until his guilt is established by the prosecution. But when an accused relies upon the 'General Exceptions' in the IPC or on any special exception or in any law defining an offence, Section 105 of the Evidence Act, 1872, raises a presumption against the accused and also places a burden on him to rebut the said presumption.

Although the jury in the sessions court had returned a verdict of not guilty, it was decided by the Supreme Court that on such a charge as in the present case, it was not possible for the jury, who were laymen, to know the exact scope of the defence and also the circumstances under which the case was made out. The Supreme Court noted that more than three hours had lapsed between K.M. Nanavati being made aware of the affair and driving to his ship to obtain a revolver with six rounds. They found that Nanavati had committed a planned and premeditated murder and, as a result, convicted him for it, awarding him life imprisonment. The Supreme Court thus concurred with the decision of the Bombay High Court.

In view of the observations made by the Supreme Court, the Government of India took the momentous decision of abolishing the jury system in India in 1960 by amending the Code of Criminal Procedure in 1973.

The verdict also caused much uproar among the public at large, fuelled by vehement tirades in Karanjia's *Blitz*.

In addition to overwhelming public interest, this case was also marked by a degree of political strong-arming. Before the final pronouncement of the life-imprisonment sentence by the Supreme Court, the then prime minister, Jawaharlal Nehru, was approached to intercede and advise the suspension of the sentence. Accordingly, the then governor of Bombay, Sri Prakasa, passed a decree ordering the suspension of the sentence and placing Nanavati under naval custody. This could easily have been construed as illegitimate use of political clout in favour of Nanavati, who was a regular in the Nehru–Gandhi circles.

In a nutshell, there were two factors that favoured Nanavati—public opinion of him as a wronged martyr and the immense support that the Indian Navy and the Bombay Parsi Panchayat exhibited. In one instance, 8500 people assembled to support the governor's decree in a rally held at Cowasji Jehangir Hall.

This case also had an impact on the case against Bhai Pratap, a freedom fighter from the Sindhi community. Charged with misusing an import licence for his sports-goods business, Pratap's case was to be scrutinized by two bureaucrats, B.B. Paymaster and R.L. Dalal. Of the two, Paymaster was Parsi. Although found innocent, it was suspected that Bhai Pratap's chances of acquittal could have been marred by the acrimony between the Sindhi and Parsi communities that the Nanavati case had created. To find a way around this, Ram Jethmalani, adviser to the prosecutor in the Nanavati case, conferred with Rajni Patel, Nanavati's defence lawyer, and Sylvia Nanavati to persuade

Mamie Ahuja to grant a written pardon to Nanavati. This took some effort, but Mamie eventually gave in. In 1962, both Bhai Pratap and Kawas Nanavati, who had been in prison for three years by that time, were pardoned by the new governor of Bombay, Vijaya Lakshmi Pandit, who was also Nehru's sister.

Nanavati moved to Canada with his wife and children shortly after his release. He never spoke publicly about the case and was hidden from the media glare till the time he passed away in 2003.

Fallouts

The main legal fallout of the case was that jury trials were given a quiet burial and removed from the statute books. In any case, jury trials had been limited only to serious criminal cases, barring a few exceptions. The argument of the abolitionists was that had jury trials been such an important component of the criminal justice system in India, then, like Australia and the US, where trial by jury is a constitutional right, the constituent assembly would have given it the same exalted status in India as well. As this was not the situation, and the experience of the Nanavati case had presented the drawbacks in the system, jury trials were excluded from the revised CrPC of 1973. Around the same time, jury trials, for their own particular reasons, were also abolished from fellow commonwealth countries like South Africa, Pakistan and Singapore.

Jury Trials in the US

Jury trials might have been abolished in India but they are still prevalent in many countries around the world, including the UK. The country where it is still most prevalent is the US, where jury trials are a common feature in both civil and criminal cases. Trial by jury in some sense has become a part of the American consciousness and to a large extent has come to define the American legal system. In any society governed by the rule of law, the dispensation of justice is of paramount importance. But to be able to do that in an effective manner, the legal system has to be free from biases and prejudices as much as possible. However, at times, there are cases where justice as envisaged by the law is at odds with the collective morality of the people. The following example serves to highlight this point very well.

The O.J. Simpson Murder Trial

The O.J. Simpson murder trial was perhaps one of the most watched events of the last decade of the twentieth century and certainly the most publicized criminal trial in American history. Simpson, an African-American former NFL star was put on trial for the murder of his white ex-wife, Nicole Brown Simpson, and a white waiter named Ron Goldman. This case again highlighted the racial fault-lines and the effect they have on the justice system. Simpson, despite substantial evidence against him, was acquitted by a predominantly black jury. In subsequent analysis, it was claimed that the jurors on arriving at a not-guilty verdict were swayed more by race considerations than actual evidence.

This trial highlights two important facts—first, that in a jury trial, a large number of people examine the same situation and that these people, drawing upon their varied experiences, offer a better chance of looking at the case from all directions to come to a final conclusion. Second, the jurors, unlike judges, are not trained to be objective in their approach and, therefore, are more likely to get swayed by extra-legal considerations such as morality.

Similarly, in the case of Nanavati, it was alleged that the jury had been swayed by extra-legal considerations of morality and the mass hysteria whipped up by Karanjia's *Blitz*, and this had led to an overturning of the decision.

Parsi Matrimonial Courts

In India, personal law is largely the domain of religious communities and sees little interference from the government. Although there have been demands from many quarters for enacting a uniform civil code, it is yet to become a reality. Given this situation, the Parsi community—which has given India illustrious personalities such as J.R.D. Tata, Homi Bhabha, Sam Manekshaw and Nani Palkhivala—continues to adjudicate their matrimonial matters by jury trial.

The system of holding jury trials for settling matrimonial disputes is unique to the Parsi community and is a good example of the past continuing to survive in the present. In this 150-year-old tradition, a five-member jury selected from a pool of twenty Parsi jurors settles matrimonial disputes between community members. The twenty members are nominated by the community council for a decade and usually consist of retirees.

The five members that constitute a jury are selected by the presiding judge through a draw of lots, but the lawyers appearing on behalf of the plaintiffs and defendants can veto a particular juror to avoid any conflict of interest.

The Parsi community, given their unique culture and history, have preserved this long-standing tradition, but not without inviting criticism. Though these trials don't deal with criminal law, they continue to represent a long-gone era of Indian history.

Conclusion

As much as we would like to see the world in Manichaean terms—black and white, good and evil— it is not possible to do so. The complexities of life often throw up situations where you cannot take a binary view. The case of Nanavati is one such situation. Like the O.J. Simpson case, the jurors in this case sympathizing with Nanavati saw justification in his actions and, therefore, held him to be not guilty.

Our rule-of-law-based society necessitates that we pick a side. One is either on the side of Nanavati, the great patriot and husband wronged by his wife's infidelity, or

Ahuja, the playboy mercilessly murdered by Nanavati for having an affair with his wife. The jurors deciding the case picked Nanavati's side. The higher judiciary, purely on the touchstone of law, found Nanavati guilty. But beyond the realm of law is the world of morality: Was Nanavati morally right in killing a man who had destroyed his marriage and family? The public opinion felt that Nanavati had been wronged, so did the jury—but not the law.

8

THE UNAFRAID: WE CALLED HER NIRBHAYA

As I was having my morning tea on 17 December 2012, a headline caught my eye—a girl had been found raped and grievously wounded on the streets of South Delhi. The news reports stated that the young woman had been raped in a moving bus and was in a critical condition. Little did I realize that morning that this gruesome incident would ignite a nation and change the way we viewed society.

Individually, we are small but integral cogs in the huge machinery that operates and controls our behaviour and our sense of morality, right and wrong. Even though as a society we have common ideas about what is acceptable or unacceptable behaviour, there are times when certain issues challenge certain notions. Then these instances are often watered down to drawing-room talk about how something terrible had happened to someone and how the system had failed him or her. At these times, I have often found people lamenting about how society is a passive onlooker to these tragedies and making a vague reference to 'something' that needs to be done.

The anger and indignation that we felt as a collective group at the gang rape and murder of a twenty-three-year-old woman became one such defining moment in our history where that vague reference to 'something' took on a more concrete form. The mass protests brought to the fore the power of the people, and to my mind questioned the reliance on already structured systems. Considered unsafe for women, the streets of New Delhi became witness to a movement so large and vehement—the likes of which have rarely been seen. The reverberations of that one incident in December 2012 are seen even as I write this, in the form of posters on buses, rickshaws and taxis. And hopefully, this would trigger a change in attitude towards brutality and objectification of women.

~

The capital of our country, New Delhi, built from seven cities, and conquered, pillaged and rebuilt over and over has accumulated a charm of its own. The streets are a mixture of the old and the new, from the shiny new colonies of South Delhi to the old-world charm of the old city, embodying the polarity between modern and traditional attitudes. On a cold December night, a twenty-three-year-old medical student from Ballia, Uttar Pradesh, was subjected to a horrific crime on the streets of this very city. What she went through that fateful night shook our very cores and her death questioned our very ability to function as a civilized society. She embodied the ideal Indian woman, planning to give free medical care to the needy, provide for her family, and change the perception that a woman can't dream big in a traditionally male-dominated society. She was the bridge between the old and the new India, one of the many young people in the country trying to break through the stifling fixity of their lives. She could have been anybody—our daughter, neighbour, friend, sister . . .

The trauma that 'Nirbhaya' underwent struck our hearts and seemed to be felt by every citizen. Not only did the incident lead to large-scale civil protests, it also led to revolutionary changes in the criminal justice system, both in a substantive and administrative manner.

A cold night in foggy Delhi saw Nirbhaya and her male friend returning home after watching the movie *Life of Pi* at a theatre in Saket, South Delhi. They tried to find an autorickshaw to take them to the outskirts of the city, and even though it was only a forty-five-minute drive, they could not find transport. Left with few options, they boarded an off-duty bus at about 9.30 p.m. from Munirka for Dwarka. It was not late at night by any reckoning; she was not out alone; and they were taking public transport—she had done all the things that women all over the world are told to do in the interest of safety.

On the bus were five other male passengers and a male driver. At first, nothing seemed out of the ordinary. But shortly after they boarded the bus, things went very wrong. The bus deviated from its normal route and its doors were shut. The driver switched off the lights. The male friend of the girl objected when three of the passengers, namely Ram Singh, Akshay Thakur and Mohammed Afroz started misbehaving, asking him why he was with the girl at this late hour: *'Tu itni raat ko ladki lekar kahan ghoom raha hai?'* An argument began and a scuffle ensued. Little did they know this was no ordinary scuffle and would end up in death and then the resurrection of humanity and our faith in it. The young man was beaten, gagged and knocked unconscious with an iron rod.

What happened next beggars description. According to newspaper reports, the bus was driven around Delhi for over an hour with its curtains drawn. The girl was mutilated, beaten and raped by the men one by one while her friend lay unconscious.

The extent of injuries was brutal, the worst being the insertion of an iron rod into her genitals. The rod, which was later recovered, was a jack handle.

After the assault, Nirbhaya and her friend were robbed and thrown out of the moving bus. The Supreme Court judgment mentions the fact that the assailants were exhorting that they should not be left alive.

Both victims lay unconscious and partially clothed on the Vasant Vihar road that connects to Mahipalpur. Several people and vehicles would have passed them, but probably due to the harassment of complainants in road accident cases, no one stopped, and they continued to lie there unclothed for almost forty-five minutes. A passer-by found them at around 11 p.m. and alerted the police, who took the couple to Safdarjung Hospital, where Nirbhaya was placed on ventilation. The extent of her injuries was such that immediate surgery was required. Unfortunately, the trauma was not yet over for her, and she had to undergo multiple surgeries. In the final operation that she underwent in India, most of her intestine was removed. The matter inflamed the public imagination to an extent that the authorities decided to send her to Singapore for treatment.

Nirbhaya was to be moved to Mount Elizabeth Hospital, a multi-organ transplant specialty centre. She was transported on 27 December. During the six-hour-long air ambulance flight, she collapsed, never to regain consciousness again.

Debates raged on news channels as to whether she was in a condition to be taking a flight. The entire nation followed the news with bated breath and hoped for recovery; I too was amongst them. A young girl was fighting for her life, and an entire country was behind her wishing and praying for her recovery, but to no avail. The girl we had all come to know as 'Nirbhaya' succumbed to her injuries at 4.45 a.m. (IST) on 29 December. Her body was cremated on 30 December in Delhi amid high security.

This extract from the Supreme Court judgment details the horrific injuries suffered: 'The trial court has recorded that the victim's complete alimentary canal from the level of duodenum up to 5 cm from anal sphincter was completely damaged. It was beyond repair. Causing of damage to jejunum is indicative of the fact that the rods were inserted through vagina and/or anus up to the level of jejunum'. Further 'the septicaemia was the direct result of internal multiple injuries'.

In the days following the incident, a Delhi-based tabloid had revealed the victim's name, for which the Delhi police registered a criminal case against the editor as disclosure of a female victim's identity is an offence under Section 228(A) of the IPC, unless the family of the rape victim agrees to it.

Soon after, the victim's father was quoted as saying, 'We want the world to know her real name. My daughter didn't do anything wrong, she died while protecting herself. I am proud of her. Revealing her name will give courage to other women who have survived these attacks. They will find strength from my daughter.'[1]

Protesters congregated on every street corner and the atmosphere was one of anger and disbelief. One of our own had been taken in a fashion that shook our very belief in the inherent goodness of human beings. The city I had spent all my life in felt unsafe for me and for my loved ones, and this fear propelled us all.

The youth of India, it seemed, had had enough. Women it seemed had had enough. Among candlelight vigils and mass silent gatherings, Delhi seemed poised to fight for their rights. The police tried to control the demonstrations by summoning the Rapid Action Force, and demonstrators faced batons, tear gas and water cannons. The extent of the movement seemed surreal to me. I have rarely seen mass protests on the scale witnessed on the streets of India those days.

The police found and arrested the suspects within a day of the crime. CCTV footage was taken from Hotel Delhi 37, which was located on the route that the bus driver had taken during the dastardly act; this helped identify the white bus with yellow-and-green stripes, a private vehicle hired by one of Delhi's schools. That led the police to Ram Singh, the driver.

Six men were arrested, including Ram Singh and his brother Mukesh Singh, who were both found in Rajasthan. Two others, Vinay Sharma, a gym instructor, and Pawan Gupta, a fruit seller, were arrested in Delhi. Akshay Thakur was arrested on 21 December from Karmalahang village in Aurangabad, and the seventeen-year-old Mohammed Afroz from Badayun, Uttar Pradesh, was arrested at the Anand Vihar terminal in Delhi. The latter had met the other perpetrators for the first time on the day of the incident itself.

The night of 12 December had started for these six with dinner at Ram Singh's house; he was an employee of Yadav Travels. They planned to drive around in the bus and try their luck at robbing somebody. Right before they picked up Nirbhaya and her friend, they had robbed a carpenter by the name of Ram Adhar.

All six were put on trial. The fight for justice was long and complicated, going on for many months. The charges were rape, kidnapping and murder. In March 2013, the bus driver Ram Singh was found hanging in his cell—by using his own clothes.

Mohammed Afroz was adjudged to be seventeen years and six months old on the day of the crime by the

Juvenile Justice Board (JJB), and even though a request for a bone ossification test was made by the police for accurate determination of his age, it was denied by the JJB. As a result, Afroz was tried separately in a juvenile court. Due to the extremely violent nature of his alleged crime, a petition seeking his prosecution as an adult was filed, but was subsequently rejected by the JJB.

He was convicted of rape and murder on 31 August under the Juvenile Justice Act. The court sentenced him to three years' imprisonment in a reform facility; this term included the eight months that he had spent in custody since the beginning of the trial. The board opined that although Afroz was involved in a heinous crime, there was no evidence that he had been the one who brutalized the girl the most, even though the charge sheet filed by the police stated so. The board cleared him of charges under Sections 307, 396 and 397 of the IPC, but found that he had committed the offence of hatching a criminal conspiracy. Despite the gruesome nature of the attack on the girl and her companion, he was released on 20 December 2015.

In mid-September 2015, the Delhi High Court was moved for stay of the release of Mohammed Afroz. The main issue before the court was 'whether a juvenile in conflict with law, who is found to have committed an offence and sent to Special Home by Juvenile Justice Board, can be released on expiry of the period of stay ordered without ascertaining the factum of reformation that is necessary for his social reintegration'. The Delhi High Court refused to order a stay on the release of the juvenile convict and was of the opinion that they could not stop the juvenile's release as per the statutory and existing provision of law. The court also asked the JJB to interact with the convict, his guardians and officials of the Delhi government regarding his post-release rehabilitation. The petitioners pointed out that the juvenile convict continued to be unreformed and indeed had become radicalized by his association with another juvenile convicted for his involvement in the Delhi High Court blast case on 7 September 2011, and that there was no material to establish the mental state of Afroz. The penal law of India is reformatory in structure, believing that reform is possible in most cases. This jurisprudence is strongly advocated when the accused is a juvenile. Afroz was released keeping in mind pro-release jurisprudence and the idea of reform of juveniles.

The Delhi Commission for Women filed a petition before the Supreme Court to prevent the release. The commission made a representation to the then chief justice requesting the setting up of a committee to visit the juvenile at the observation home to assess his current mental condition. It was pleaded that under Rule 32 of the Delhi Juvenile Justice (Care and Protection) Rules, 2009, long-term institutional care as a last resort should be permitted. However, the Supreme Court upheld the decision of the high court.

The trial of the remaining four suspects was fast-tracked by the Saket court and within ten months—a record time in the context of Indian judicial pace—they were declared guilty and given capital punishment.

The Delhi High Court upheld the death penalty on 13 March 2014, placing the case in the class of 'rarest of rare category' which provides for capital punishment.

On 5 May 2017, the Supreme Court too upheld the death sentence against the accused. A three-judge bench, comprising Justice Dipak Misra, Justice R. Banumathi and Justice Ashok Bhushan expressed their anguish by stating that the incident created a tsunami of shock.

The report said:

We are here concerned with the award of an appropriate sentence in case of brutal gang-rape and murder of a young lady, involving most gruesome and barbaric act of inserting iron rods in the private parts of the victim. The act was committed in connivance and collusion of six who were on a notorious spree running a bus, showcasing as a public transport, with the intent of attracting passengers and committing crime with them. The victim and her friend were picked up from the Munirka bus stand with the mala fide intent of ravishing and torturing her. The accused not only abducted the victim, but gang-raped her, committed unnatural offence by compelling her for oral sex, bit her lips, cheeks, breast and caused horrifying injuries to her private parts by inserting iron rod which ruptured the vaginal rectum, jejunum and rectum. The diabolical manner in which crime was committed leaves one startled as to the pervert mental state of the inflictor. On top of it, after having failed to kill her on the spot, by running the bus over her, the victim was thrown half naked in the wintery night, with grievous injuries.

Ramachandran, the amicus curiae (a person appointed by the court to assist it in a particular matter) appointed by the Supreme Court, opposed the sentence on the count that mitigating circumstances should have been taken into consideration. The court took a stringent view and said:

I have considered all the aggravating and mitigating circumstances in the present case. Imposition of appropriate punishment is the manner in which the courts respond to the society's cry for justice against the crime. Justice demands that the courts should impose punishments befitting the crime so that it reflects public abhorrence of the crime. Crimes like the one before us cannot be looked with magnanimity. Factors like young age of the accused and poor background cannot be said to be mitigating circumstances. Likewise, post-crime remorse and post-crime good conduct of the accused, the statement of the accused as to their background and family circumstances, age, absence of criminal antecedents and their good conduct in prison, in my view, cannot be taken as mitigating circumstances to take the case out of the category of 'rarest of rare cases'. The circumstances stated by the accused in their affidavits are too slender to be treated as mitigating circumstances.

The present case clearly comes within the category of 'rarest of rare case' where the question of any other punishment is 'unquestionably foreclosed'. If at all there is a case warranting award of death sentence, it is the present case. If the dreadfulness displayed by the accused in committing the gang-rape, unnatural sex, insertion of iron rod in the private parts of the victim does not fall in the 'rarest of rare category', then one may wonder what else would fall in that category.

The impact of the incident was such that it jolted the entire machinery into action—it was as if someone had flicked on a bulb. A mere six days after the incident, a committee headed by a former judge of the Supreme Court, J.S. Verma, was set up to consider and suggest changes in the criminal law and make it deterrent in nature. The committee was given thirty days to submit its report. Contrary to precedence, the committee prepared its report in twenty-nine days after considering more than 80,000 suggestions and petitions received by them from the public, jurists, lawyers and various other factions of the society. The report found that crimes against women were directly linked to failures of the government and the police. The major suggestions of the report were to make rape punishable by life sentence instead of death as it had been seen that the death sentence did not act as a deterrent, and clearing ambiguity over the control of the Delhi police in such cases. The committee, however, did not favour setting the official age of a juvenile at sixteen rather than eighteen.

The Criminal Law (Amendment) Act, 2013, also expanded the definition of rape to include oral sex as well as the insertion of an object or any body part into a woman's vagina, urethra or anus.

The punishment for rape is seven years at the least and may extend up to life imprisonment. Any man—be it a police officer, medical officer, army personnel, jail officer, public officer or public servant—who commits rape may be imprisoned for at least ten years. A punishment of life imprisonment, extending to death, was prescribed for situations wherein the rape concludes with the death of the victim, or the victim being in a vegetative state. Gang rape has been prescribed a punishment of at least twenty years under the newly amended sections.

The new amendment defines 'consent' to mean an unequivocal agreement to engage in a particular sexual act; clarifying further that the absence of resistance will not imply consent. Non-consent is a key ingredient for commission of the offence of rape.

Thus the brutal gang rape of 2012 led to key structural changes in the way the judiciary now interprets rape laws. Age-old ideas of 'habitual of sex' and 'vaginal penetration' have been replaced by structures that respond more accurately to how women experience sexual assault. It overrides the chauvinistic mindset of only 'vaginal-penile' penetration, and targets 'natural' and 'unnatural' penetrative assault of any nature under the same umbrella.

The widespread public outrage against the juvenile's release after three years was mirrored by the victim's parents, who felt that justice had not been served, and releasing the boy who had committed such a heinous act would encourage others of his age to commit such crimes. This led the legislators to propose a change in the laws relating to juveniles. The Juvenile Justice Bill 2015 was introduced before both the houses of the Parliament, with a proposal in the bill to consider those between sixteen to eighteen years of age as adults. The bill was debated in the Rajya Sabha extensively, with the government hoping to pass the bill in spite of having no majority. The Lok Sabha passed the bill on 7 May 2015. The Juvenile Justice (Care and Protection of Children) Act, 2015, came into force on 1 January 2016.

In 2012, Save Life Foundation filed a Public Interest Litigation (PIL) in the Supreme Court, requesting it to safeguard Good Samaritans who come forward to help the injured. This issue came into the limelight again after this gruesome incident. That night no one had come to the rescue of the victims. They were lying on the street grievously hurt and partially naked. People in cars, autos and other vehicles passed them, but none of them rushed to help and take the victims to the hospital. This level of apathy was alarming. The ministry of road transport and highways notified guidelines for the protection of Good Samaritans in May 2015.

What Went Wrong?

As a hired school bus, the vehicle was not permitted to be on the road at the time of the incident. Had the system been better and the authorities more vigilant, the incident wouldn't have taken place at all. Also, police vans reached the victims forty-five minutes after they were thrown from the bus.

The Delhi government did take certain serious steps to remedy the situation, but it took two years to do so. By 2014, GPS tracking systems were installed in 6321 Delhi Transportation Corporation (DTC) buses, 45,000 autos and 5549 chartered buses. But the only overall measure that was successful to a certain extent was the DTC's night-service system, which increased its capacity from forty-two to eighty-five buses in the year 2014.

In 2015 the Central government released Rs 125 crore from its Nirbhaya Fund for installation of CCTV cameras in DTC buses. A year later, the transport ministry issued a draft notification, making it mandatory for all transport vehicles with a seating capacity of over twenty-three passengers to have CCTV cameras connected to GPS, so as to be monitored by the local police control room. In the recent railway budget, Rs 700 crore has been allocated from the Nirbhaya Fund towards the installation of CCTVs in trains, specifically long-distance ones.

Gender inequality is the primary tumour of our society, and rape, trafficking, child marriage, female foeticide and honour killings the metastases. I believe that in India, the problem is not a lack of laws, but the manner in which they are implemented.

Four and a half years later, the 'Nirbhaya case' is a touchstone of almost mythical proportion. No single crime has resulted in as much lawmaking and law-amending as this one. The Nirbhaya judgment, to some extent, will assuage a sense of retributive public justice. In a country where justice has always been delayed, the pronouncement of this judgment in a time-bound manner may serve as a ray of hope. And with the launch of the Good Samaritan law, there is the expectation citizens will step forward and help those in need. Another Nirbhaya would not have to lie helplessly on the roads of this country.

Many have opposed the death penalty awarded in this case, but as rightly said by Justice Banumati, it was a 'barbaric crime' that shook the conscience of the nation and 'question of any other punishment is unquestionably foreclosed'.

For me, the day the sentence was given marked a palpable, tangible difference in the way we view victims of sexual assault. For once, the outpouring of emotion had to do with anger and there was no victim shaming. The rage was felt not just by the kin of the victim, but by the whole society, especially women, who are at a higher risk of becoming victims. I saw society change and imbibe the values that we as women lawyers have fought for decades to bring to the fore. Sadly, the cost was very high, a young life cut short in its prime.

9

THE BUTCHER OF NITHARI

Normally, crimes are identified with criminals, but sometimes the places where they are committed become synonymous with the incident. Nithari is a small village in Noida. Hitherto insignificant, it sprang into prominence between 2004 and 2006, when several children were reported missing in the area. The villagers had complained to the police multiple times about this pattern, but to no avail. The Noida police were merely silent spectators. They seemed more keen on keeping the cases off the books and chalked the missing children reports to children eloping with their lovers.

On 29 December 2006, two Nithari residents sought the help of former Resident Welfare Association (RWA) president S.C. Mishra as they claimed to have found the location of the remains of children who had gone missing over the last two years. Upon a search, in a tank drain in D block, directly behind house no. D-5, a decomposed hand was found. By the time the police arrived, the local residents had found three partial skeletons in the drain.

These events led to a national furore that came to be known as the 'Nithari Kaand'.

More and more decomposed remains were dug up. The decomposed bodies were identified as those of children who had gone missing over the last two years. There were nineteen skulls in all, sixteen intact and three damaged. The post-mortem reports showed that eleven of the victims were girls or women. Doctors at the Noida Government Hospital found that there was a 'butcher-like precision' in the chopping of the bodies. Each body had been cut into three pieces before being disposed of. It was alleged that the accused, after strangulating the victims, would sever their heads and throw them in the drain behind the house. The viscera would be stored in a polythene bag before being discarded.

In January 2007, the residents of D-5 were arrested. They were identified as Moninder Singh Pandher—the owner of the house and Surendra Koli—the domestic help.

The media latched on to the case and carried out a trial by itself, convicting the two.

Multiple theories were put forward by the media houses. One was that these children were prostitutes, whom Koli would procure for the master of the house, Pandher. After he was satiated, together they would kill them and deal with the bodies in a gruesome manner so as to get rid of the evidence.

Some believed that there was an international child pornography racket being run from the residence by both the men. This was partially supported by the fact that the investigating teams seized erotic literature, along with a laptop connected to a webcam from the house. The police also recovered some photographs of Pandher with nude children and foreigners, taken during his international visits.

Yet another theory was that the murders were committed for organ trade. The police even raided the house of a doctor who lived in the neighbourhood, on the basis that the doctor had been accused of a similar crime in 1998, although the court absolved him later that same year. This theory was also canvassed by the senior defence counsel Ram Jethmalani during the review petition against the death penalty in the Supreme Court, where I had appeared on behalf of the government. Jethmalani's attempt to use this argument to exonerate his client from the death penalty failed and the case was dismissed.

Ultimately, it was revealed that it was Surendra Koli who had committed the gruesome crime. Taken into custody on 29 December 2006, he spilled the beans during interrogation and confessed to having slain several women and children in the house, chopping their bodies into small pieces and throwing them into the drain behind the house. Koli also stated that these crimes had been carried out of his own volition and that Pandher had had no role to play in the crimes.

Despite investigation by the CBI, no hard evidence or proof was found against Pandher. During one of the murders, he was said to be in Australia, while during others, he was thought to be in Chandigarh. Due to the lack of evidence, the CBI claimed that no charge sheet could be filed against Pandher, effectively giving him a clean chit. Of course, in law, a charge sheet or a closure report is not the final word. The court can take a different view. In this case, the trial court disagreed with the closure report and summoned him.

This clean chit is not without controversies of its own. It has been alleged time and again that Pandher was an influential man, with multiple politicians frequenting the D-5 residence before the events took place. It is said that he used his considerable connections to get rid of all the evidence against him. These allegations have been made by the media time and again. As the matter is still sub judice before the Supreme Court, I do not want to comment on these allegations. I seek only to inform of the proceedings as they took place in court and the reasons Pandher was convicted and subsequently acquitted.

In the trial court, both the accused were ultimately charged and tried for murder, rape, criminal conspiracy and kidnapping.

Multiple cases were filed for crimes committed against each victim. These cases are pending in various courts. I shall restrict my focus to the Rimpa Haldar case as the charges brought against the two sum up all the other cases as well.

The investigation found that on the pretext of offering work, Koli and Pandher would call a woman or child inside the house and rape and strangulate her or him. After that, they would murder the victim with an axe or a knife. Then to destroy the evidence, they would cut up the body into small pieces and throw them into the drain behind D-5.

Both accused denied the charges in the trial court. They pleaded that they had been falsely implicated and claimed to be innocent.

Eventually, the trial court convicted Surendra Koli on the following grounds:

1. A knife, chappal, purse, skulls and bones recovered on 29 December 2006.
2. Koli was in the habit of standing outside the house and luring in girls and children on the pretext of arranging work or other attractions.
3. Comparison of the DNA of the relatives of the victims and that recovered from the skulls and bones helped identify the victims and their families.
4. A fairly accurate demonstration of the procedure of cutting of bodies as carried out by Koli.
5. Another knife recovered on 11 January 2007.
6. An axe recovered on 8 January 2007.
7. The confessional statement of Surendra Koli was crucially incriminating.

The following is a chilling extract from the confessional proceedings of Surendra Koli on oath before the magistrate, translated from the Hindi:

'Okay. Yes. The road in front of the house leads to Nithari village . . . The address is D-5 Sector 31. I had been working there since July 2004. After work, I used to stand at the gate. I don't entirely remember but I think it happened in 2005. Yes, beginning of 2005, maybe in January or February. I was alone at home at that time and a girl was going in the direction of Nithari from Sector 30. Later on, I got to know that her name was Rimpa. I called her inside for work. When she came inside, I told her . . . I would talk to madam regarding the pay . . . Yes, and when she started looking inside the house, I used her *chunni* and strangulated her from behind. She fell unconscious. Then I tried having sex with her. After trying for a while, when I was not able to have sex with her, I killed her by strangulating her again with her chunni.'

'Okay, why did you kill her?'

'Such pressure had been built in my mind that I should cut her and eat her. Then, right after that, I took her to the bathroom. At that time, there was no fear in my mind that somebody would come home or something would happen or a scene would be created. I mean there was no fear as such . . . Then I took her to the bathroom upstairs. Then I went downstairs. I went to the kitchen and fetched a knife . . . At that time itself, I cut her and ate an arm and a piece of her chest.'

'Okay.'

'Yes, I cooked it in the kitchen . . . itself.'

'Cooked it in the kitchen?'

'Yes. I don't clearly remember how much I ate in the evening. In the evening, at around 4–5, when I was completely satiated, I saw that her slippers and everything were lying in the drawing room itself. Till then, there was no realization. It was as if I was drunk. I don't consume anything like alcohol, paan, cigarette, beedi, gutkha, nothing at all. Okay. So such feelings arose in my mind like I should cut somebody and eat. Then, after a couple of days, somewhere around a month, I ate the same girl so much after evening that my mind was satisfied. Then I went to the bathroom upstairs and saw that her body, cut into pieces, was lying all over the place. At the time of cutting, I had not realized what I had done to her. After that, out of fear, I quickly wrapped her into polythene packets and kept her in the bathroom. Then at night, I washed everything and kept her in the gallery which is there behind the house and where nobody would come. I threw her in that gallery.'

The confessional statement and the recoveries made on the basis of this statement made up the bulk of the case against Koli. The trial court found him guilty and sentenced him to death.

However, the case against Pandher is not so cut and dried. There was no such confession. The trial court convicted him on the basis of circumstantial evidence, holding that the number of body parts recovered and the smell arising from them was no less than that of a slaughterhouse and would spread over a large distance. Therefore, it would be impossible for a person living in the house to have no knowledge of the bad smell.

The trial court also believed that Koli was motivated to commit such criminal activities because he was influenced by Pandher's promiscuous activities of having two or three call girls over at a time. Being a witness to these probably made Koli want to have sex with the girls, and also kill them and eat their organs.

The trial court held that Pandher and Koli had collaborated on the murders. The court discounted the evidence that Pandher had been in Australia at the time Rimpa was murdered and held that it had not been proved beyond reasonable doubt by the accused. Circumstantial evidence was enough to convict Pandher. The trial court awarded the death penalty to both Koli and Pandher.

On appeal in the Allahabad High Court, Koli's sentence was upheld. However, in a move that shocked the national media and public, the decision against Pandher was reversed, and he was acquitted.

It was contended that Pandher was in Australia from 30 January 2005 to 15 February 2005, while Rimpa was murdered on 8 February 2005. The court deduced that it was not possible for Pandher to have been involved in the murder. Credence was given to the alibi furnished by his wife, Devender Kaur, who said that Pandher was with her in Australia from 30 January 2005 to 15 February 2005. Her testimony remained unchallenged. However, if the family's sources are to be believed, Devender Kaur had a strained relationship with Pandher and they had separated. She lived with her son who was stationed in Canada. The counsel for the complainant also raised questions regarding the absence of documentary evidence like Pandher's air tickets or other travel documents. The high court, however, rejected the complainant's contention, and gave credence to Pandher's alibi.

The high court referred to the confessional statement which revealed that a girl or a woman would be murdered every forty-five days or so and her body parts would be thrown into the drain. And before these body parts could decompose, another murder would be committed. It was observed by the high court that it was beyond comprehension how this circumstance could be reckoned to be incriminating to Pandher. It was also noted that there was no such evidence on record that the foul smell spread over a distance of 1 kilometre—in fact, there was no evidence of a foul smell at all. During the investigation of the case, several persons had visited D-5 and no one had spoken about any foul smell pervading the house. It was clarified that Surendra Koli, as per his confessional statement, used to throw the body parts after wrapping them up in polythene and, therefore, there was little chance of a foul smell.

It was also revealed in the confessional statement that Surendra Koli, prior to joining Pandher's service, had worked in several houses but had never been charged with such offences. The high court theorized, just like the trial court, that the reason for this was the lubricious behaviour of Pandher. He used to bring two or three girls to his house and revel in drinking and having sex with them. Watching Pandher indulging in such activities, the high court hypothesized, criminal propensity and lust accentuated in Koli, leading him to commit these gruesome murders. The confessional statement demonstrated that when Pandher was not bringing in the girls, Koli had no distraction, but when Pandher did, he was inclined towards murder.

The high court, however, opined that the acts of debauchery by Pandher could hardly be taken as 'incriminating circumstance' that attracts the provision of Section 120B of the IPC which lays down the punishment for criminal conspiracy. There are certain basic ingredients that constitute criminal conspiracy. They are: (a) an agreement between two or more persons; (b) the agreement must relate to doing or causing to be done by either: (i) an illegal act or (ii) an act which is not illegal in itself but is done by illegal means. Therefore, the meeting of minds of two or more persons for doing or causing an illegal act to take place or an act carried out through illegal means is sine qua none of criminal conspiracy. The high court relied on the confessional statement and found no link or meeting of minds between Pandher and Koli to get Rimpa Haldar inside the house and commit the offences. Needless to say, in Koli's confessional statement, no allegation was made against Pandher. There was not an iota of evidence to attract the provision of Section 120B of the IPC or Section 30 of the Evidence Act, which provides that a confessional statement by one person would act against others too if they are being tried jointly for the same offence. The entire incriminating circumstance was based on the confessional statement of Koli. The high court also pointed out that the sessions judge could not cull any inculpatory part from Surendra Koli's statement which leaned against Pandher. The only thing construed unfavourably was that Pandher used to bring girls to his house, one of whom was named Payal, but because of a lack of evidence, the court acquitted Pandher of Rimpa's murder.

The court observed, 'We can fully understand that though the case, superficially viewed, bears an ugly look so as to prima facie shock the conscience of any court, yet suspicion however great it may be, cannot take the place of legal proof. A moral conviction, however, strong or genuine cannot amount to a legal conviction supportable in law.'

Comments on the Death Penalty

The high court still had to decide whether to award the death penalty to Surendra Koli. The death penalty is only given in the rarest of rare cases. A comparative study of the arguments advanced across the bar led to the observation that on the one hand, the death penalty was considered inhumane, and on the other, the parents of an innocent girl wanted such a punishment for the abominable wrongdoing of the lustful ravishers. The court lamented that the incident was indeed 'shocking, tragic, lachrymose, hair-raising, and heart-rending'.

The mitigating circumstances discussed were that the appellant was the father of two children and had a family; however, upon consideration of the totality of circumstances, even such factors could not exempt the accused from liability. The high court thus affirmed the sessions court's order and awarded the death penalty to Surendra Koli.

Supreme Court

The Supreme Court upheld the decision of the high court to sentence Surendra Koli to death because it was 'rarest of the rare case' where a death sentence could be awarded. The bench of justices Markandey Katju and Gyan Sudha Misra confirmed the death sentence of Koli. At the same time, the Supreme Court kept the CBI appeal against the acquittal of Pandher pending, stating that any order passed against him or in his favour could have a bearing on the remaining cases, which were still at the trial stage. The bench said that before deciding on the CBI's appeal, it would wait for the outcome of the trial of other cases in which Pandher had been accused, along with Koli. The victim Rimpa's father, Anil Haldar, filed an appeal challenging Pandher's acquittal and sought restoration of the death sentence awarded to him by the sessions court, which is still pending.

On 3 September 2014, the court issued the death sentence for Koli. On the evening of 4 September 2014, Surendra Koli was transferred to Meerut jail because of the absence of facilities to execute such a penalty at Dasna jail in Ghaziabad. He was to be hanged on 12 September 2014. The Supreme Court of India stayed the death sentence for one week after a petition was filed. On 29 October 2014, the Supreme Court bench headed by Chief Justice H.L. Dattu rejected the review petition against the death sentence, stating that the court had not committed any error in judgement.

Surendra Koli's hanging was stayed at the last minute by the apex court, which decided to hear his right to plead against the death sentence in an open court. However, the Supreme Court finally rejected the petition on 29 October 2014, clearing the way for his execution. But this was not the end. A mercy petition was filed, as the People's Union for Democratic Rights (PUDR) approached the Allahabad High Court through a PIL. On 28 January 2015, the high court bench headed by Chief Justice D.Y. Chandrachud and Justice P.K.S. Baghel commuted the death sentence of Surendra Koli to life imprisonment on the grounds of 'inordinate delay' in deciding his mercy petition. The high court highlighted the delay of three and a half years in the disposal of his mercy petition by the Uttar Pradesh governor and the President, and termed the sentence 'unnecessary and unreasonable.' The court in its order held that the manner in which an execution warrant was issued for Koli by the special CBI court of Ghaziabad was in 'violation' of Koli's 'right to due process'. It also noted that Koli was kept in solitary confinement since the beginning of his conviction, which is illegal under the law.

While the death penalty still exists as a punishment in India for the rarest of rare cases, there are certain safeguards to ensure human rights: the high court is required to confirm the death sentence; as per other landmark judgments such as in the cases of Kartar Singh and Bachan Singh, it can only be awarded in the rarest of rare cases; a review petition could be filed; and Article 72 gives the President of India and the governors the right to grant pardons and to suspend, remit or commute sentences. Recently, more safeguards have been added. Inordinate delay, as in Koli's case, led to the commuting of the death sentence to life imprisonment.

Do we actually truly subscribe to the death penalty? Such a question needs to be dealt with in great detail. Though

India allows for the death penalty as a punishment, it has to be emphasized that it can only be awarded in the rarest of rare cases, as per the principle laid down by the Supreme Court in *Bachan Singh v. State of Punjab*. Deciding what constitutes the rarest of rare cases in itself is a subjective proposition. The debate is not merely a legal one. It has aspects of morality and rectitude closely intertwined with it. While some argue that the death penalty is cruel, inhumane and degrading, others are of the view that it enshrines the detrimental theory of punishment and prevents crime by instilling fear in the mind of a prospective offender. On the one hand, it can be regarded as revenge masquerading as justice, and on the other, it's a social necessity.

More than ten cases are still pending against both Pandher and Koli at various stages of trial and appeal. Only time will tell us the outcome of these cases.

However, in all this the media has reincarnated itself as the public court. It has been the voice of the people who can never be heard, the light to the people who can never see the reality and the guide to the judge effecting the decisions. High-profile litigation is not just decided in the courts; it is also decided in the court of public opinion. The magnitude of the coverage and the filter through which the media reports on litigation can create a 'clear bias'.

Yet, as I mentioned in other chapters, media scrutiny is often positive and seeks to undo the injustices that status and wealth can unleash. As far as issues pertaining to court litigation are concerned, it is for the readers to form their own views.

10

ELECTED TO DEATH

The idea of political assassinations is antithetical to the idea of democracy. The entire premise of electing a person representing a particular idea or ideology to run a state is defeated when, for political reasons or ideological clashes, these leaders become a target of violence.

The term 'assassination' is generally understood as the murder of a prominent personality, usually a political leader or ruler, and is, sadly, an age-old concept. Instances of assassination are as old as the institution of governance itself, and can be traced as far back as ancient Egypt. In its long, dark history, it has manifested in the form of filicide, patricide and matricide, and the killings of the leaders of political parties, thinkers and philosophers. Murder has often created rulers and changed dynasties, and these killings are then rewritten in the word and in favour of the victor as 'tributes', as liberation from a harsh rule or freedom from tyranny.

We all have different ideals, identify with separate factions and tend to disparage or disregard conflicting theories. Intolerance towards these different ideas manifests in various ways, but assassination is the worst form of intolerance, often used as a motive to drive home an almost-fanatical show of power. An assassination sends the message 'We are more powerful than you' in order to prove power, to prove that one faction is better, and sometimes to exact revenge or prevent the leader from doing something the assassins don't want him to do. A key difference between the assassinations of pre-Independence India and post-Independence India is that in the former, political assassination as a tool of political censorship has not been very frequent. In fact, most assassinations have been carried out by radical separatists or breakaway faction groups or rebellions.

One of the biggest shocks our country received was within a year of Independence, when India had to cope with the assassination of the 'father of our nation', Mahatma Gandhi, by a fanatical extremist. Mahatma Gandhi was on his way to address a prayer meeting at Birla House, when he was shot at point-blank by Nathuram Godse, who allegedly held Mahatma Gandhi responsible for Partition, which arose in the process of attaining Independence. Considering that Gandhi was widely regarded as almost a saint with extremely clean, untainted intentions, his assassination was a shock, and the question resounded: Who would want to kill a proponent of ahimsa?

Yet again, in 1975, when the country was grappling with nationwide protests and high rates of inflation and unemployment, Lalit Narayan Mishra, the then railway minister was assassinated at the Samastipur railway station while inaugurating the Broad Gauge Link. The trial court noted that the assassin's motive was to pressurize the government to release the leader of Anand Marga, who had been arrested on charges of murder. The trial for the case was finally concluded on 8 December 2014, resulting in the conviction of the four accused. This was the first case that had been transferred outside a state in order to ensure that no tampering of evidence took place.

However, the case that shook the conscience of the country was that of the assassination of the then prime minister Mrs Indira Nehru Gandhi. In 1984, the incumbent PM, Mrs Gandhi, was killed by the very men stationed to protect her. On the morning of 31 October she was fired upon by her bodyguards in retaliation to the army's Operation Blue Star—the infamous military action taken to strike at the roots of the militancy movements in the Punjab area. The strike was carried out to attack the militants who had hidden in the Golden Temple at Amritsar.

In 1991, political heir and the eldest son of Indira, Rajiv Gandhi, was assassinated while campaigning for the ongoing general elections. He was killed by a suicide bomber affiliated to the Liberation Tigers of Tamil Eelam (LTTE) because he sent the Indian Peace-Keeping Force (IPKF) to Sri Lanka in 1987. In 1995, yet another political leader, the then Punjab chief minister Beant Singh was assassinated by a suspected Khalistani separatist in a car blast at the Secretariat Building, Chandigarh. In this chapter, I will dwell on the Rajiv Gandhi assassination case and the trial that ensued.

The Assassination of Rajiv Gandhi

India has always been a diverse state. While we mostly take pride in it, the other side of the coin presents an ugly reality. As a nation, we have been grappling with militancy in various parts of the nation, from Kashmir to south India.

The group that organized the assassination of Rajiv Gandhi was the LTTE. Under the leadership of V. Prabhakaran, the LTTE came into existence in 1976. Eventually, the movement became an anti-establishment one, and the Sri Lankan government adopted stern measures to curb the organization's activities. A series of confrontations took place between the government and the LTTE activists. In an attempt to end the civil war situation that had been created in Sri Lanka, the then PM of India Rajiv Gandhi signed an Indo-Sri Lanka Accord on 29 July 1987. The LTTE was among the signatories of this accord. As a result of this agreement, the Indian government sent the IPKF to Sri Lanka to disarm the LTTE.

It is alleged that the IPKF committed atrocities against the Tamilians in Sri Lanka and that the Indian government did not cooperate with the LTTE. The IPKF was finally recalled in March 1990. Before the 1991 general elections, Rajiv Gandhi said in an interview that if he returned to power, he would consider resending the IPKF to Sri Lanka. This enraged the LTTE and the organization, in retaliation, planned to assassinate Rajiv Gandhi.

The LTTE made up its mind to prevent Gandhi from regaining power, even if it required assassinating him. Realizing that he would be a near-impossible target as the prime minister, it was decided that they would strike while his security status was still that of the leader of the Opposition, as election campaigning would render him vulnerable.

The nefarious scheme was put into action on 21 May 1991, when Rajiv Gandhi arrived at around 10 p.m. to an election meeting at the town of Sriperumbudur in Tamil Nadu. He was surrounded by people trying to garland him. A sub-inspector on duty, Ansuya, tried to prevent a woman called Dhanu, an undercover LTTE suicide-squad member, from getting close to Rajiv. She had almost caught hold of the assassin, but was interrupted by Gandhi, who, according to Ansuya, had wanted everybody to get a chance to meet him. Dhanu bent down, as if she wanted to touch Rajiv Gandhi's feet. The latter, in turn, bent to lift her up. It was just at this moment that Dhanu detonated the battery-operated belt bomb strapped around her waist and concealed under her clothes. She, together with Haribabu, a photographer engaged by the LTTE to take photographs of the horrific sight, died in the blast. Rajiv Gandhi lost his life, along with fifteen people, including nine policemen. Forty-three others suffered injuries.

A charge of conspiracy was framed under TADA, the IPC, the Arms Act, 1959, the Telegraphy Act, 1933, the

Foreigners Act, 1946, the Explosive Substances Act, 1908, and the Passports Act, 1967, against a total of forty-one persons, out of which twelve were already dead, having committed suicide, and three were absconding. The remaining twenty-six faced trial before the special TADA court. S. Nalini, T. Suthendraraja (alias Santhan) and Sriharan (alias Murugan) were Accused nos. 1, 2 and 3.

A total of twenty-five charges were framed against the accused. Under Section 15 of the TADA, confessions were recorded by the Superintendent of Police, CBI/Special Protection Group, who had been deputed in the Special Investigation Team. The special court convicted all the twenty-six accused and awarded the death penalty to all. The court referred the case to the Supreme Court for the confirmation of the death sentence for all the convicts.

In the appeal,[1] the Supreme Court confirmed the death sentences of Nalini, Santhan and Murugan. On the other hand, the death sentences of Robert Payas (alias Kumaralingam), S. Jayakumar (alias Jayakumaranand) and P. Ravichandran (alias Ravi) were altered to life imprisonment. The conviction of the other accused under Section 302 of the IPC was set aside. All the charges under Sections 3(3), 3(4) and 5 of TADA were also set aside by the Supreme Court.

The apex court held that the act was not punishable under the TADA as there was no motive to overawe the government, and neither was Rajiv Gandhi a member of Parliament nor was he under oath to protect. A senior leader of the LTTE had personal animosity towards Rajiv Gandhi, which had led to cadres of the LTTE developing hatred towards him. This was so because Rajiv Gandhi was associated with the atrocities allegedly committed by the IPKF in Sri Lanka.

Nalini and the other accused in the matter made a confessional statement, giving complete details of how the plan was executed and who had been involved. One of the dilemmas of the Supreme Court was how to examine these statements and to what extent they were admissible in evidence.

The TADA was a legislation made specifically to curb terrorist activities; it was often considered draconian, sometimes bypassing the controls and checks that are part of the Indian Evidence Act, 1872, and overriding it. In the matter of confessions, where the latter act has mandated that the confessions made to a police officer are not admissible, the TADA mandates the admissibility of such confessions.

When Section 15 of the TADA states that the confession of an accused, if voluntary and valid, is admissible against a co-accused, it would be taken as substantive evidence against the co-accused. When it comes to deciding the value that is to be attached to a confession, that will be determined by the appreciation of the evidence. As a matter of prudence, the court may look for some corroboration if a confession is to be used against a co-accused, though that will again be within the sphere of appraisal of the evidence.

It was contended before the Supreme Court that the killing of Rajiv Gandhi was not a terrorist act and hence not punishable under Section 3 of the TADA. The court accepted this contention as there was no intention seen to overthrow the government or perform a terrorist activity. The court held that even though the TADA was not applicable to the matter at hand, the confessions would still hold merit as the trial had taken place under the same. The Supreme Court held:

> The aforesaid implications of Section 12 vis-à-vis Section 15 of the TADA have not been adverted to in Bilal Ahmed's case. Hence, the observations therein that 'while dealing with the offences of which the appellant was convicted there is no question of looking into the confessional statement attributed to him, much less relying on it, since he was acquitted of the offences under TADA' cannot be followed by us. The correct position is that the confessional statement duly recorded under Section 15 of the TADA would continue to remain admissible as for the other offences under any other law which too were tried along with TADA offences, no matter that the accused was acquitted of offences under TADA in that trial.

The court analysed the merit of the matter divorced from the public prejudice and held that the TADA would not apply in the case. The governing law was held to the IPC and the court convicted the persons accused for offences under the IPC as against the TADA.

The court observed:

> Though we have held that [the] object of the conspiracy was not to commit any terrorist act or any disruptive

activity, nevertheless the murder of a former Prime Minister for what he did in the interest of the country was an act of exceptional depravity on the part of the accused, an unparalleled act in the annals of crimes committed in this country. In a mindless fashion not only that Rajiv Gandhi was killed along with him others died and many suffered grievous and simple injuries.

The objectivity with which the Supreme Court delivered the judgment in a high-stakes case shows how deeply the rule of law and constitutional values are embedded in India. The fact that it was an Indian prime minister that had been assassinated did not impact or take away from the rigour of the rule of law and deciding the governing law.

Recent Controversy

In 2000, Nalini's death penalty was commuted to life imprisonment by the governor of Tamil Nadu on the basis of a recommendation by the state cabinet and a public appeal by Sonia Gandhi, the widow of Rajiv Gandhi.

The three death-penalty convicts in the Rajiv Gandhi assassination case also filed a petition in the Supreme Court.[2] The court, while reiterating the principles laid down in Shatrughan Chauhan's case, held that delay makes the process of execution of the death sentence unfair, unreasonable, arbitrary and capricious and thereby violates procedural due process guaranteed under Article 21 of the Constitution. The Supreme Court held in this landmark case, 'Like the death sentence is passed lawfully, the execution of the sentence must also be in consonance with the constitutional mandate and not in violation of the constitutional principles.' A dehumanizing effect on the victims is presumed in such cases, regardless of the actual suffering that the delay caused. Considering the fact that long delays in cases of capital punishment mentally torture the accused, as they alternate between hope and despair, the death sentences of the three convicts were commuted to rigorous imprisonment for the remainder of their lives, subject to any remission granted by the appropriate government.

The controversy did not end there. The then Tamil Nadu chief minister Jayalalitha's government wrote a letter to the Central government in 2014, making a recommendation to release all seven convicts in the case. There was a threat of the state government going ahead with the release, irrespective of the Central government's views. The Central government approached the Supreme Court contending that under the CrPC, only the Central government was empowered to commute the sentence and release the convicts.[3] The matter was referred to a constitutional bench of the Supreme Court.

The bench held[4] that it is mandatory for the state government to consult the Central government. Moreover, the opinion of the Central government would be given primacy over the opinion of the state government. The decision to grant remission must be well informed, reasonable and fair, and the opinion of the presiding judge of the court before which the conviction was confirmed must be sought. The court also stated that a special category of sentence instead of death can be substituted by the punishment of imprisonment for life or for a term exceeding fourteen years, which can be put beyond application of remission by the court.

Political Assassination: A Global Phenomena

Ever since the Moabite King Eglon was stabbed to death on his throne in 1200 BCE, and probably even long before that, political leaders have been killed for any number of reasons.

The logic of political assassinations is distinct from that of other manifestations of violence. The state is mostly a major actor in these cases. Consequently, it is not surprising that Opposition leaders are more likely to be targeted in authoritarian systems or in weak democracies where the political environment provides space for the emergence of opposition.

The former chairperson of the Pakistan People's Party, Benazir Bhutto, was Pakistan's first and, till date, only female prime minister. She was the eldest child of the former prime minister of Pakistan, Zulfikar Ali Bhutto. On 27 December 2007, Bhutto was killed while leaving a campaign rally for her party at Liaqat National Bagh in the city of Rawalpindi. After entering her white Toyota Land Cruiser, a bulletproof vehicle, Bhutto stood up through its sunroof to wave to the crowds. At this point, a gunman fired shots at her. This was followed by the detonation of explosives near the vehicle, which killed approximately twenty people. Bhutto was critically wounded and rushed to hospital, where she was declared dead.

John F. Kennedy, the thirty-fifth President of the United States, served from 1961 until his death in 1963. Winning by a narrow margin in the popular vote, Kennedy became the first Roman Catholic President. On 22 November 1963, when he was hardly past his first thousand days in office, Kennedy was killed by an assassin's bullets as his motorcade wound through Dallas, Texas. Kennedy was the youngest man elected President and also the youngest to die.

Martin Luther King, an American clergyman, activist and prominent leader in the African-American civil rights movement is a national icon in the history of modern American liberalism. On 4 April 1968, a shot rang out as King stood on the motel's second-floor balcony. The bullet entered through his right cheek, smashing his jaw, then travelled down his spinal cord before lodging in his shoulder. After emergency chest surgery, King was pronounced dead. King's autopsy revealed that though only thirty-nine years old, he had the heart of a sixty-year-old man, perhaps a result of the stress of thirteen years in the civil rights movement. The assassination led to a nationwide wave of riots in more than a hundred cities.

Abraham Lincoln, nicknamed Honest Abe, was the sixteenth President of the United States from March 1861 until his assassination in April 1865. The assassination of Abraham Lincoln took place on Good Friday, 14 April 1865, as the American Civil War was drawing to a close. The assassination occurred five days after the commander of the Confederate Army of Northern Virginia, General Robert E. Lee, surrendered to Lieutenant General Ulysses S. Grant and the Union Army of the Potomac. Lincoln was the first American President to be assassinated, though an unsuccessful attempt had been made on Andrew Jackson thirty years earlier in 1835.

Thomas D'Arcy McGee, an Irish nationalist, Catholic spokesman, journalist and the father of the Canadian Confederation, also met with the same fate. On 7 April 1868, McGee participated in a parliamentary debate that went on past midnight. Then he went home and, while waiting for his landlady to open the door, he was purportedly assassinated by Patrick J. Whelan. Whelan, a Fenian sympathizer and a Catholic, was accused, tried, convicted and hanged for the crime.

～

Looking at such political assassinations, the question arises: Why are political changes prompted by killing specific individuals and not by other means? There are varied opinions in this regard. The offenders may believe that such an assassination is the fastest way to promote their interests. Another reason can be that other alternatives are not viable, forcing the perpetrators to consider assassination. It may even be the case that the political assassination is only a stage in the scheme devised by the offender to fulfil an agenda. Whatever the precise reason may be, the offender does see a causal relationship between the assassination and advancement or the prevention of certain policies.

What cannot be discounted is that the impact of such assassinations is enormous. They shake the very foundation of a country, causing a decline in the democratic nature of a state and increasing instability.

The world today is highly volatile. The TV and the media constantly remind us of this upheaval that our society is undergoing. The rise of power blocs in today's world is becoming more dangerous than before. The world is changing at breakneck speed, and however much we try and contain this, the chaos that we are entering into is undeniable. In these times we look towards our leaders and our chosen elected representatives to show us the way and give us direction. I strongly believe we need stronger governments than ever before to protect us and our leaders from becoming victims.

11

THE TANDOOR MURDER CASE

What began as a regular night on 2 July 1995 for constable Abdul Nazir Kunju and home guard Chanderpal of the Delhi police turned into one of the most enduring cases in the Indian criminal justice system. The two were patrolling the area of Ashoka Road Western Court in Delhi, when they encountered a panicked woman screaming at the top of her lungs that the Bagiya restaurant in Hotel Ashok Yatri Niwas had been set on fire.

Expecting a fire, they rushed to the spot near the Janpath Lane where the hotel is situated and scaled the wall to enter the premises. The scene that awaited them would spark nightmares across the nation. Unfortunately, this did not seem to be a regular fire. Something was burning in the eatery's tandoor (a type of clay oven).

Tending to the fire was the manager Keshav Kumar and Sushil Sharma, co-owner of the place; they were seen placing wooden logs and small pieces of firewood into the burning fire, stoking it. On being asked what was burning, the manager claimed he was a Congress worker burning old banners and posters, but the two policemen smelled a foul odour and detained the two.

What awaited them when they doused the fire was something they would never have expected on that balmy July night. The tandoor was stuffed with partially burnt human remains, a torso and burnt bones. A black polythene sheet nearby bore traces of blood.

The body was eventually revealed to be that of twenty-nine-year-old Naina Sahni, the wife of the co-owner, the one stoking the fire in the tandoor. She had been brutally slaughtered by her better half, the then Delhi Youth Congress president Sushil Sharma.

The police quickly apprehended Kumar, but Sharma managed to escape them. In view of the disclosure statement made by Kumar, the police started investigating and raided Sharma's apartment in Gole Market. They found blood as well as a bullet mark embedded in the plywood and shell casings. A diary was also recovered in which was written: 'Naina Sahni loves Sushil Sharma'. The blood, bullets and the diary seemed to point towards a love story gone very wrong.

As indicated by the charge sheet put together by the police, Sharma and Sahni had begun to live together, which had led to a secret wedding. However, all was not right and Sharma started believing that his new bride was having an illicit affair with her schoolmate and close colleague in the Congress party, Matloob Karim. The suspicion prompted considerable discord, and, the police said there was abusive behaviour on the part of Sharma at home. Keeping the marriage a secret was also putting a strain on the newly-weds. This was on Sharma's insistence, as he believed news of his marriage would negatively impact his political career.

The chain of circumstances which led to Sahni's death began on 2 July, when Sharma reached his home at Mandir Marg in the heart of the capital. He found Sahni chatting on the phone and consuming alcohol. Upon seeing him, she immediately put down the phone. Sharma redialled the number to find out whom she was talking to. His worst fears were confirmed when Karim answered at the other end. Enraged, Sharma shot Sahni using a .32-bore revolver. One shot went through her head, another hit her in the neck, while the third missed her and hit an aeration-and-cooling system.

Sahni died on the spot. What happened next makes one's stomach churn. Sharma wrapped the body and took it to Bagiya Restaurant, where he hacked his wife's body into pieces and, thereafter, with the help of Kumar, attempted to burn the body in the tandoor to get rid of any evidence. During the investigation, when Sahni's body was shown to her parents, they were so distraught that they could only cry and were unable to identify the body. The body was finally identified by the same Matloob Karim, who had been accused of having an affair with the victim. The post-mortem examination revealed that the burn injuries were posthumous in nature.

Sharma, in the meanwhile, had fled to Bombay and then to Madras. Upon finding out about his arrest warrant, he applied for anticipatory bail in the sessions court in Madras, which was granted to him, but later rejected by the Madras High Court. Sharma was later arrested in Bangalore by the local police on 10 July and handed over to the Delhi police on 11 July. On investigating the hotel room where the accused had stayed, they found a .32-bore revolver, four live cartridges and some other documents.

A second autopsy was also conducted. It was concluded upon an X-ray examination that there was one lead bullet in the skull and one in the neck of the deceased. The cartridges found in the flat of the accused and the lead bullets found in the body of the deceased were sent to the Central Forensic Science Laboratory, and were confirmed to have been fired from the same revolver. They also found a kurta with the blood of the deceased on it.

The use of the tandoor to attempt to cover up the murder is what truly horrified people and made this become a case people could not stop talking about. Not many people remember that the tandoor was not the weapon of the murder, that Naina had been shot to death and the tandoor was only used to destroy the body.

The Supreme Court categorically admits that there is a very thin line between awarding the death penalty and a life sentence. The manifest arbitrariness evident on the face of the record in Supreme Court judgments has time and again invited the ire of scholars. The Sushil Sharma verdict exemplifies the cause of this dilemma. This case primarily revolved around two key issues. Firstly, it highlights the importance of a false plea of alibi in weakening the case of the accused. Secondly, it analyses the submissions made by the petitioner and respondent regarding the sentencing of the accused and concludes that the facts and circumstances of the case allowed the Supreme Court to reduce the punishment from the death penalty to sentence unto life, subject to remission allowed.

The second issue is what makes this case significant in the context of the prioritization of mitigating factors while determining whether a case is one of death penalty. This case is unique for prioritizing the nature of the criminal over the nature of the crime while sentencing. It becomes necessary in the context to examine the sociological and legal foundations of this judgment, and to answer the larger question of the nature of the imposition of penalties in cases involving brutality in crime.

The following two questions were the highlights of this case, which we will delve into as well:

1. Should the focus of the death penalty be the nature of the crime or that of the criminal?
2. What factor(s) should be prioritized while deciding between life sentencing and the death penalty?
   A. Is the age of the accused a mitigating factor?
   B. Is there a possibility of reform in the present case? To what extent is the possibility of reform to be prioritized?
   C. To what extent is brutality in the murder an obstacle to mitigating the sentence of the accused?

The Trial

The trial was held in the sessions court in Delhi where Sharma pleaded that due to the media furore and the misdirected public hatred he would be subjected to an unfair and unjust trial. Therefore, he claimed, he should either be discharged or the trial be postponed. On being denied the relief he sought, he then appealed to the Delhi High Court, which found that the media exposure did not prejudice the accused. The petition was dismissed.

Justice Thareja awarded capital punishment to Sharma, placing the case in the 'rarest of rare' category, warranting the imposition of the extreme punishment. Interestingly, Justice Thareja, who had convicted Sharma for being guilty beyond doubt, had earlier had to acquit a man he believed was guilty in the Priyadarshini Mattoo murder case. Sharma's accomplice, Keshav Kumar, the restaurant manager at the time, was sentenced to seven years' rigorous imprisonment for criminal conspiracy. Jai Prakash Pehalwan, Rishi Raj Rathi and Ram Prakash Sachdeva, accused of sheltering Sharma after the murder, were acquitted for want of evidence.

During the course of the trial, hordes of media persons turned up at the Tis Hazari court. A group of about fifty protesters entered the court premises with a tandoor and demanded the death penalty for Sharma.

In December 2013, the Delhi High Court admitted an appeal filed by Sushil Sharma, challenging his conviction and death sentence by the trial court. A division bench of Justices Vijender Jain and R.C. Jain also admitted for hearing the reference sent by the trial court.

Sharma had sought to get the order of the additional sessions judge G.P. Thareja reversed on the grounds that the trial court failed to appreciate the evidence on record, which did not support the prosecution case. He also made his case that 'the sessions court failed to appreciate that there was no evidence to support the use of firearms in the murder. The case is based on circumstantial evidence but the link connecting the accused with the crime is missing at several points'. Sharma also made references regarding Matloob Karim's vested and conflicting interest in the case. However, the high court rejected these assertions and upheld the verdict of the trial court in this case.

On the other hand, the Supreme Court saw the case differently. Holding that the homicide by Sushil Sharma of his significant other was the result of a strained individual relationship and not an offence against society, the Supreme Court commuted the capital punishment to life imprisonment for whatever was left of his life.

The Supreme Court first analysed the case at hand and reached the conclusion that the accused are indeed liable to be convicted for committing the heinous crime of murder and brutally disposing of the body of the accused. Thereafter, it examined whether or not it would be appropriate to award the death penalty, given the facts and circumstances.

To determine the same, the court took into consideration various judgments laid down by it in the past to understand the circumstances in which the death penalty has been awarded instead of a mere life sentence to the accused. The court referred to one such past judgment[1] in which the accused had committed seventeen murders in five incidents, occurring in the same night in quick succession in five neighbouring villages, as a result of a family feud, with the motive of reprisal. Some of the accused were sentenced to death. The Supreme Court also referred to the judgment of the constitution bench in the case of Bachan Singh and culled the following propositions as emerging from Bachan Singh's case:

(i) The extreme penalty of death need not be inflicted except in the gravest cases of extreme culpability.

(ii) Before opting for the death penalty, the circumstances of the 'offender' also require to be taken into consideration along with the circumstances of the 'crime'.

(iii) Life imprisonment is the rule and death sentence is the exception. In other words, the death sentence must be imposed only when life imprisonment appears to be an altogether inadequate punishment, having regard to the relevant circumstances of the crime, and provided, and only provided, the option to impose sentence of imprisonment for life cannot be conscientiously exercised having regard to the nature and circumstances of the crime and all the relevant circumstances.

(iv) A balance sheet of aggravating and mitigating circumstances has to be drawn up and in doing so the mitigating circumstances have to be accorded full weightage, and a just balance has to be struck between the aggravating and the mitigating circumstances before the option is exercised.

It was further observed that to apply these guidelines, the court must ask and answer the following questions:

(a) Is there something uncommon about the crime which renders the sentence of imprisonment for life inadequate and calls for a death sentence?

(b) Are the circumstances of the crime such that there is no alternative but to impose the death sentence even after according maximum weightage to the mitigating circumstances which speak in favour of the offender?

Considering the facts of the Tandoor murder case, the court made the following observations in light of the mitigating factors, while determining whether or not the death penalty should be awarded. Firstly, it said that the offence at hand had not been one against the society. Since the accused had no previous criminal record and there is no evidence suggesting that he would resort to such crimes in the future, it was possible that the accused would be rehabilitated and reformed if allowed the opportunity to do so. Moreover, it held that brutality alone cannot be grounds for awarding the death penalty to an individual.

The Supreme Court regarded the criteria enshrined in the case of Bachan Singh,[2] where it had, while relying upon another judgment rendered by the US Supreme Court,[3] held that in the presence of the following aggravating circumstances, the court may impose the penalty of death in its discretion:

(a) if the murder has been committed after previous planning and involves extreme brutality; or

(b) if the murder involves exceptional depravity.

I believe that the possibility of reform may also be determined by the conduct of the accused. When a person commits a crime that crosses a moral threshold, which the collective conscience of the society deems as morally reprehensive and deplorable, in such situations, it would be incorrect to prioritize the need for reform over the need for punishing the perpetrator proportionately. In this case, the decision that reform is possible in the present case seemed to be based on considerations such as the fact that the accused was weeping in the mortuary upon seeing the dead body.[4]

In *Subramaniam Swamy v. Union of India*, the Supreme Court held that although there is no satisfactory definition of a crime, the word would embrace all acts and omissions which are criminal, and would affect the security or well-being of the public generally. A crime is a moral wrong which is inimical to the general moral sense of the community. In fact, the court also admitted in the following words:

A crime affects the society. It causes harm and creates a dent in social harmony. When we talk of society, it is not an abstract idea or a thought in abstraction. There is a link and connect between individual rights and the society; and this connection gives rise to community interest at large. It is a concrete and visible phenomenon. Therefore, when harm is caused to an individual, the society as a whole is affected and the danger is perceived.

The Supreme Court, quoting Kenny's,[5] admitted that any conduct that harms an individual to some extent *also* harms the society to some extent, since a society is a collection of individuals.

Be that as it may, I believe that the Supreme Court, in the tandoor murder case, rightly rejected the plea for the death sentence. This individualistic approach to criminal jurisprudence is not only humane but is completely in consonance with sound legal principles already established.

The Law Commission of India, in its 264th Report, under Paragraph 7.2.4, recommended that although retribution plays an important role in punishment, it cannot be reduced to vengeance. The Law Commission has also consistently maintained that the death penalty is not an effective deterrent. The same has been echoed by agencies of the United Nations and NGOs such as Amnesty International.

In the Tandoor murder case, the heinous act of the accused of not only murdering the victim but also going ahead and attempting to dispose of her dead body is deplorable to the highest degree. The court, however, evaluated the crime in its essence, away from the societal baying for blood in keeping with a sound jurisprudential legacy. A case for a murder is never a simple crime; it always encompasses myriads of human emotions. As students of law, it falls on us to separate the wheat from the chaff; the quantum of punishment does not just depend on the crime but also on the circumstances around it, including whether it was an isolated incident, an unpremeditated result of provocation, or whether the accused showed remorse.

Upon a perusal of a variety of Supreme Court judgments, it is apparent that there is always a huge debate about awarding the death penalty. The Death Penalty Research Project, undertaken by researchers at the National Law University in New Delhi, found that over 80 per cent of prisoners facing capital punishment had not completed school and nearly half had begun working before the age of eighteen. While in the Nirbhaya judgment, the Supreme Court completely disregards the age of the accused while determining the possibility for reform, in the Tandoor murder case, the Supreme Court had done the exact opposite by duly regarding age as a factor.

The court's decision in examining not just the letter of the law but also the circumstances surrounding the crime has given true meaning to the letter and spirit of 'rarest of rare'. The land of the Mahatma has, in its essence, 'reform' as a building pillar to its penal system. The tandoor murder case is an example of this. Sushil Sharma was a first-time offender, and if the entire matter is viewed objectively, discounting the public ire involved, the matter in its essence was simple murder. The idea that inflamed public prejudice was the barbaric manner in which the body had been disposed of. That the verdict judiciously dealt with the tragedy speaks volumes about the conscientiousness of the society at large, and how it is distinctly removed from that of a barbaric mob.

NOTES

CHAPTER 2: WOMEN WHO KILL

1. Candace Sutton, 'Serial killer sisters Renuke Shinde and Seema Gavit who abducted and murdered children in bid to avoid execution at the gallows', News.com. au, 22 April 2017, http://bit.ly/2wYEAf3.

CHAPTER 3: A TWIST OF FATE: THE YOUNG ONES

1. *State v. Jasbir Singh @ Billa and Kuljeet Singh @ Ranga* ([1980] 17 DLT 404).
2. *Kuljeet Singh v. Union of India* ([1981] 3 SCC 324).
3. *Kuljeet Singh alias Ranga and Anr. v. Lt.-Governor of Delhi and Ors* (AIR 1982 SC 774).
4. *Prabha Dutt v. Union of India* ([1982]) 1 SCC 1).

CHAPTER 4: BLOODLESS MURDER: DEFAMATION

1. (2012) 7 SCC 288.
2. (2013) 10 SCC 591.
3. (2010) 5 SCC 600.
4. AIR 2006 SC 2522.
5. AIR 2015 SC 1523.
6. (2016) 7 SCC 221.

CHAPTER 6: IN THE NAME OF GOD: TERRORISM

1. (1996) 1 SCC 478.

CHAPTER 8: THE UNAFRAID: WE CALLED HER NIRBHAYA

1. Gaurav Vivek Bhatnagar, 'Disclosing the Identity of Rape Victim Remains a Grey Area in the Justice System', Wire.in, 28 July 2016, http://bit.ly/2hBcKzD.

CHAPTER 10: ELECTED TO DEATH

1. *State of Tamil Nadu v. Nalini & Ors* [1999] 5 SCC 253).
2. *V. Sriharan alias Murugan v. Union of India* ([2014] 4 SCC 242).
3. *Union of India v. V. Sriharan and Ors* ([2014] 11 SCC 1).
4. WP (CRL) 48 of 2014.

CHAPTER 11: THE TANDOOR MURDER CASE

1. Under paragraph 63 of the judgment, it looks at *Machhi Singh*, a three-judge-bench decision.
2. *Bachan Singh v. State of Punjab* ([1980] 2 SCC 684).
3. *Furman v. Georgia* (33 L Ed 2d 346 : 408 US 238 (1972).
4. Para 83 of the judgment.
5. *Kenny's Outlines of Criminal Law*, 19th Edition, 1966, by J.W. Cecil Turner.